networks™

Florida
SOCIAL
STUDIES

Florida Studies

McGraw
Graw
Hill
Education

Program Authors

James A. Banks, Ph.D.
Kerry and Linda Killinger Endowed
  Chair in Diversity Studies and
  Director, Center for Multicultural
  Education
University of Washington
Seattle, Washington

Kevin P. Colleary, Ed.D.
Curriculum and Teaching Department
Graduate School of Education
Fordham University
New York, New York

Linda Greenow, Ph.D.
Associate Professor and Chair
Department of Geography
State University of New York at
  New Paltz
New Paltz, New York

Walter C. Parker, Ph.D.
Professor of Social Studies Education,
  Adjunct Professor of Political
  Science
University of Washington
Seattle, Washington

Emily M. Schell, Ed.D.
Visiting Professor, Teacher Education
San Diego State University
San Diego, California

Dinah Zike
Educational Consultant
Dinah-Might Adventures, L.P.
San Antonio, Texas

Contributing Authors

James M. Denham, Ph.D.
Professor of History and Director,
  Lawton M. Chiles, Jr., Center for
  Florida History
Florida Southern College
Lakeland, Florida

M.C. Bob Leonard, Ph.D.
Professor, Hillsborough Community
  College
Director, Florida History Internet
  Center
Ybor City, Florida

Jay McTighe
Educational Author and Consultant
McTighe and Associates Consulting
Columbia, Maryland

Timothy Shanahan, Ph.D.
Professor of Urban Education &
  Director, Center for Literacy
College of Education
University of Illinois at Chicago

Academic Consultants

Tom Daccord
Educational Technology Specialist
Co-Director, EdTechTeacher
Boston, Massachusetts

Joe Follman
Service Learning Specialist
Director, Florida Learn & Serve

Cathryn Berger Kaye, M.A.
Service Learning Specialist
Author, The Complete Guide to Service
  Learning

Justin Reich
Educational Technology Specialist
Co-Director, EdTechTeacher
Boston, Massachusetts

Clifford E. Trafzer
Distinguished Professor of History
Rupert Costo Chair in American Indian
  Affairs
University of California, Riverside

K. Tsianina Lomawaima, Ph.D.
School of Social Transformation
Arizona State University
Tempe, Arizona

Clara A Martinez, Ph.D.
Naco Research Institute
Social Sciences Research
Mancos, Colorado

Teacher Reviews

Karen S. Cangemi
Fourth Grade Teacher
Oakhurst Elementary
Largo, Florida

Margaret Claffey
First Grade Teacher
Jerry Thomas Elementary
Jupiter, Florida

Lisa March Folz
Fifth Grade Teacher
Blackburn Elementary
Palmetto, Florida

Amanda Hicks
National Board Certified Teacher,
  Elementary Education
Second Grade Teacher
Hollywood Hills Elementary
Hollywood, Florida

LaKeitha N. Jackson
K–12 Literacy Coach
Fort Pierce Magnet School of the Arts
Fort Pierce, Florida

Kimberly B. Kieser
Third Grade Teacher
Woodlawn Elementary

Mc Graw Hill Education

Copyright © 2018 McGraw-Hill Education

Send all inquiries to:
McGraw-Hill Education
Two Penn Plaza
New York, New York 10121

ISBN: 978-0-02-114679-6
MHID: 0-02-114679-9

Printed in the United States of America.

17 18 19 20 21 22 QSX 23 22 21 20 19

Florida's Land and Early People

BIG IDEA Location affects how people live.

My Book

My Computer

networks™

Go online and find this interactive map of Florida.

EXplore! UNIT 2 Exploration and Colonization of Florida

BIG IDEA 💡 People's actions affect others.

My Book

My Computer

networks™

Go online and find videos to learn more about early exploration.

Keep going!
Next we'll explore Florida's early history!

Explore! UNIT 3 Florida's Early History

BIG IDEA Conflict causes change.

My Computer

networks™

Go online and find
this interactive Venn
diagram.

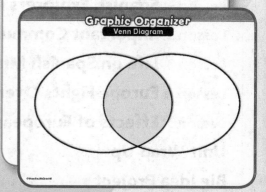

Graphic Organizer
Venn Diagram

Explore! UNIT 4 Florida in Modern Times

BIG IDEA Change happens over time.

My Book

My Computer

networks™

Go online and find this interactive map of railroads in Florida.

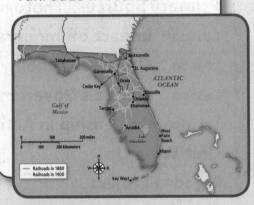

Keep going!
Next we'll explore Florida's people, economy, and government!

 **Explore! UNIT 5** Florida's People, Economy, and Government

BIG IDEA Culture influences the way people live.

My Book

My Computer

networks™

Go online and find videos about life in Florida.

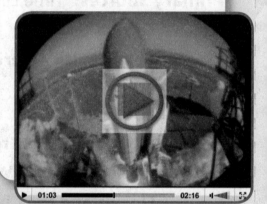

01:03 02:16

Explore! Skills and Maps

The Civil War in Florida

ATLANTIC OCEAN
Marianna 1864
Pensacola
Tallahassee
Olustee 1864
Fernandina
Fort Pickens 1861
St. Marks
Lake City
Jacksonville
Natural Bridge 1865
St. Augustine
Gainesville 1864
Cedar Key
Gulf of Mexico
FLORIDA
Tampa Fort Brooke 1863
Lake Okeechobee
Fort Myers
0 50 100 miles
0 50 100 kilometers

Capital city
Battle
Other city
Union blockade

N W E S

Key West

UNIT 1

Florida's Land and Early People

BIG IDEA Location affects how people live.

How would you describe Florida to somebody who's never been here before? You might say that the state is mostly flat and full of rivers and lakes. You might also say that the weather is usually warm and sunny. In this unit, you'll learn about the physical features, cities, tourist attractions, and weather of Florida. You'll also learn how our state's geography impacted the very first people who lived here—the Native Americans. As you read, think about the ways that location has affected people in the past and how location still impacts your daily life today.

netw⊕rks

There's More Online!
- Skill Builders
- Vocabulary Flashcards

After Lesson 1:
- ☐ Write a title at the top of the map.
- ☐ On the map legend, add the symbols used on the map for cities and the capital.
- ☐ Label the compass rose with cardinal and intermediate directions.
- ☐ Find the map scale and label it.

After Lesson 2:
- ☐ Label the Atlantic Ocean, Gulf of Mexico, Lake Okeechobee, the St. Johns River, the Suwannee River, the Apalachicola River, and the Everglades.
- ☐ Label the cities of Tallahassee, Jacksonville, Orlando, Miami, Tampa, and Pensacola.
- ☐ Choose three tourist attractions to add to the map. Create a symbol for each one and add them to the map where they are located. Add your symbols to the map legend.

After Lesson 3:
- ☐ Write a summary of the weather in Florida in the box labeled "Florida's Weather."

After Lesson 4:
- ☐ Add labels to the map to show where Florida's Native American tribes lived.

© GOODSHOOT/JUPITERIMAGES FRANCE / Alamy

Show As You Go!

Fold page here.

After you read each lesson in this unit, come back to these pages and complete the activities on the left. You will use these pages to help you complete a project at the end of the unit.

Map Legend

☐ City

☐ Capital

0		50		100
0		50	100	

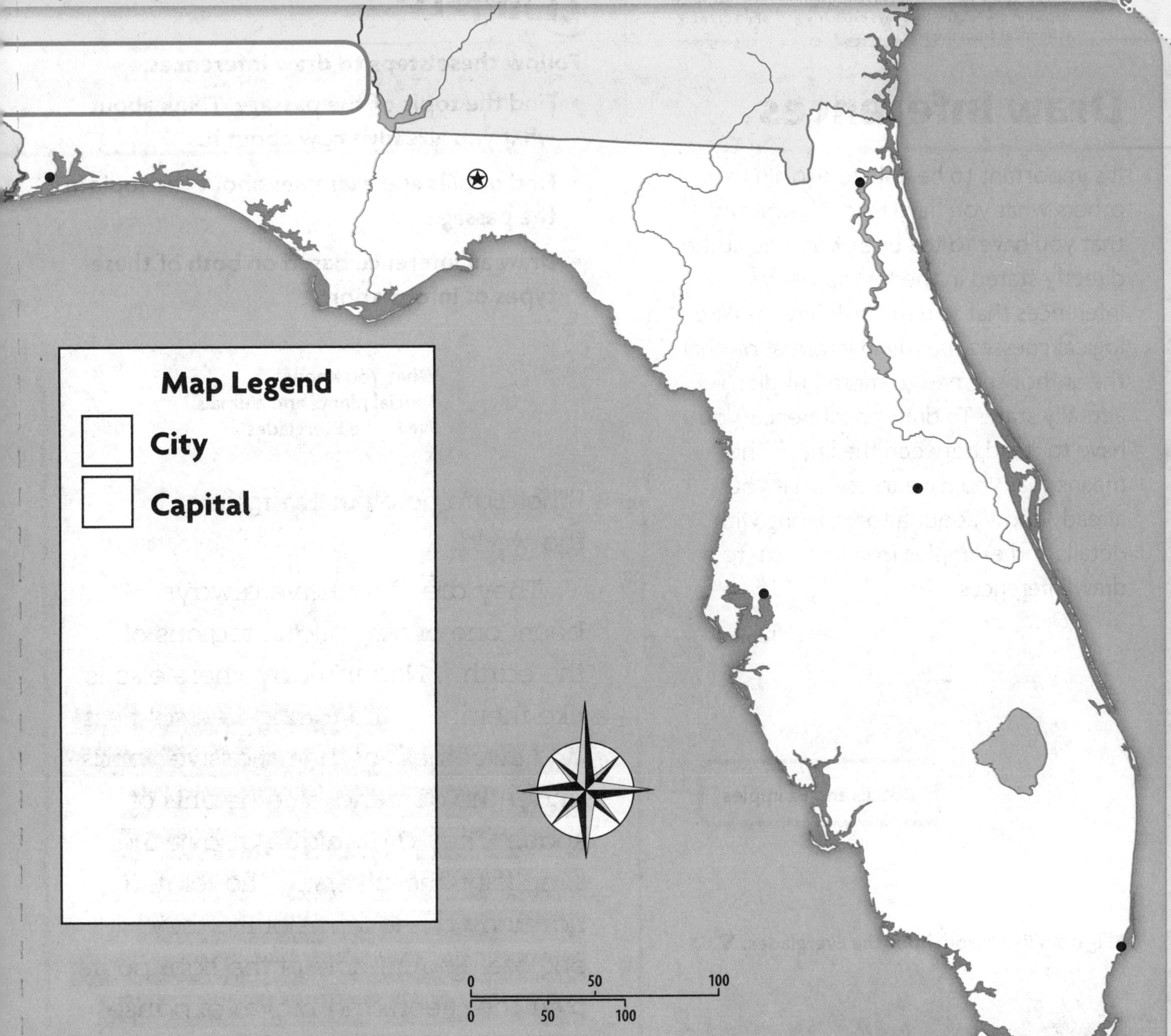

Florida's Weather

_____

_____

_____

_____

NGSS Standards
SS.4.G.1.1 Identify physical features of Florida.
SS.4.G.1.2 Locate and label cultural features on a Florida map.

3

Reading Skill

NGSS Standards
LAFS.4.RI.1.1 Refer to details and examples in a text when explaining what the text says explicitly and when drawing inferences from the text.

Draw Inferences

It's important to be able to explain to others what you have read. This means that you have to tell both what the author directly stated in the text as well as inferences that you made. Inferences are logical guesses that fill in information that the author seemed to mean but didn't actually state. To draw an inference, you have to "read between the lines." This means that you have to use what you already know about a topic, along with details and examples from the text, to draw inferences.

Topic

Details and Examples

Alligators live throughout the Everglades. ▼

LEARN IT

Follow these steps to draw inferences:

- **Find the topic of the passage. Think about what you already know about it.**
- **Find details and examples about the topic in the passage.**
- **Draw an inference based on both of these types of information.**

> **What You Know**
> Special plants and animals live in the Everglades.

"There are no other Everglades in the world.

They are, they have always been, one of the unique regions of the earth... Nothing anywhere else is like them: . . . the racing free saltness and sweetness of their massive winds, under the dazzling blue heights of space. They are unique also in the simplicity, the diversity, the related harmony of the forms of life they enclose. The miracle of the light pours over the green and brown expanse of saw grass and of water, shining and slow-moving below, the grass and water that is the meaning and the central fact of the Everglades of Florida. It is a river of grass."

—Marjory Stoneman Douglas, *Everglades: River of Grass*

Photo: (c) The McGraw-Hill Companies - Inc./Barry Barker - photographer   Text: From The Everglades: River of Grass by Marjory Stoneman Douglas. 60th Anniversary edition copyright © 2007 Pineapple Press, Inc.

TRY IT

Use the graphic organizer below to help you draw inferences.
Fill it in with information from the passage on page 4.

What You Know	Text Details and Examples	Inferences

APPLY IT

- Review the steps for drawing an inference.
- Read the passage below. Write what you already know about the topic in the box.
- Circle details and examples about the topic in the passage.
- Write your inference(s) in the box.

Do you like to collect seashells? If so, make sure you visit Sanibel Island on your next vacation! This small island off the western coast of Florida has many attractions to keep you busy. You can visit the Bailey-Mathews Shell Museum, and relax and swim at the beach. The island also has a national wildlife refuge. You might like to go for a bike ride on one of the island's trails too.

Sanibel Island ▶

What You Know:

_____

_____

_____

Inference(s):

_____

_____

_____

Words to Know

The list below shows some important words you will learn in this unit. Their definitions can be found on the next page. Read the words.

longitude (LAHN • juh • tood) (p. 14)

strait (STRAYT) (p. 17)

landform (LAND • form) (p. 17)

tourist (TUR • ihst) (p. 22)

precipitation (prih • sih • puh • TAY • shuhn) (p. 25)

drought (DRAUT) (p. 26)

midden (MIH • dihn) (p. 31)

fertile (FUHR • tuhl) (p. 33)

FOLDABLES

The **Foldable** on the next page will help you learn these important words. Follow the steps below to make your Foldable.

Step 1 Fold along the solid red line.

Step 2 Cut along the dotted lines.

Step 3 Read the words and their definitions.

Step 4 Complete the activities on each tab.

Step 5 Look at the back of your Foldable. Choose ONE of these activities for each word to help you remember its meaning:

- Draw a picture of the word.
- Write a description of the word.
- Write how the word is related to something you know.

▲ Crops can die during a drought.

Photodisc / Superstock

Lines of **longitude** measure distance east or west of the Prime Meridian.	What smaller word is within the word *longitude*? Write it below.
A **strait** is a narrow passage of water between two larger bodies of water.	What is a homophone of the word *strait*? (A homophone is a word that sounds the same but is spelled differently.)
A **landform** is a shape of land on Earth's surface.	Write two examples of landforms.
A **tourist** is a person who travels for fun.	What is the root word of *tourist*?
Precipitation is any water that falls to Earth.	Circle the examples of precipitation. snow sky clouds tornado rain sleet
A **drought** is a long period without rain.	Write an antonym for the word *drought*.
A **midden** is a trash pile of shells, bones, and other items.	Circle the words that belong with the word *midden*. mound garbage Native Americans shells valley lake
Fertile means good for growing.	Write a sentence using the word *fertile*.

FOLD

longitude	longitude
strait	strait
landform	landform
tourist	tourist
precipitation	precipitation
drought	drought
midden	midden
fertile	fertile

CUT HERE ✂

8

Primary Sources

NGSS Standards
SS.4.A.1.1 Analyze primary and secondary sources to identify significant individuals and events throughout Florida history.

Learn about Florida through primary and secondary sources!
Primary sources are written or made by someone who witnessed an event. They teach us about people, places, and events.

In contrast, secondary sources are sources that are written or made after an event happens. Secondary sources include encyclopedias, biographies, textbooks, and other books.

Maps

A historical map can be a primary source. A historical map shows what an area looked like at a particular time in the past. Maps can be secondary sources too. For example, maps made today that show what a place looked like long ago are secondary sources. Maps, both primary and secondary ones, help you understand the past.

You can see many different kinds of maps in an atlas. An atlas is a book of maps. You can find an atlas at the back of this book.

(t) Photodisc. / Superstock. (b) Courtesy of the State Archives of Florida

 Document-Based Questions

Look at the map to the right. It was made in 1594. Use it to answer the following questions.

1. What locations do you think are shown on this map?

_____

_____

2. Is this map a primary source? Why or why not?

_____

_____

networks
connected.mcgraw-hill.com
● Skill Builders
● Resource Library

Lesson
1

Using Maps

? **Essential Question**

How do maps help us understand places?
What do you think?

_____

_____

_____

_____

_____

Hi! My name is Ernesto. I love to travel, so it's important that I know how to read maps. Otherwise, I could get lost really fast! In this lesson, I'm going to help you learn all about maps. Have you used a map before? What did you use it for?

_____

_____

Maps show us all kinds of information. They can show us how to get from one place to another. They can show the location of a city, state, or country. Maps help us learn about other places too.

Words To Know

Look at the words below. Tell a partner what you already know about these words.

map legend

cardinal directions

intermediate directions

compass rose

*indicate

map scale

latitude

longitude

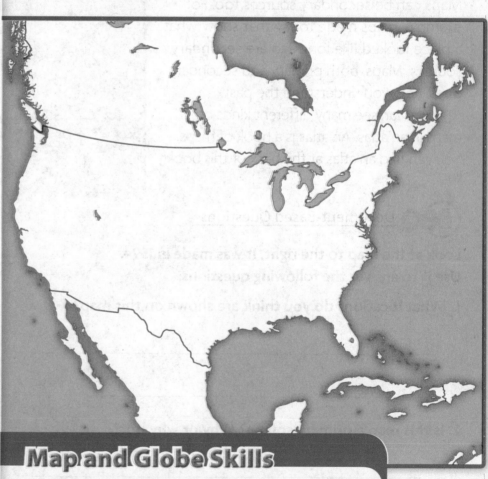

Map and Globe Skills

1. Label and color each country on the map. Look in the Atlas at the back of the book if you need help.

2. (Circle) your state and label it.

NGSS Standards
SS.4.A.1.2 Synthesize information related to Florida history through print and electronic media.

Map Elements

Maps can show a lot of information all at once, so it's important for maps to have titles. Just like the title of a book, the title of a map tells you what the map is about.

Another important part of a map is the **map legend**, also called a map key. A map legend tells what the symbols and colors on the map mean. Some maps have just a few symbols, like the one below. Other maps can have many symbols.

NGSS Standards
SS.4.G.1.2 Locate and label cultural features on a Florida map.
SS.4.G.1.4 Interpret political and physical maps using map elements (title, compass rose, cardinal directions, intermediate directions, symbols, legend, scale, longitude, latitude).

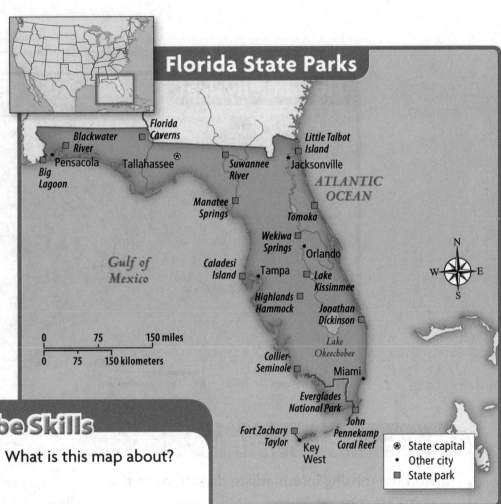

Florida State Parks

Florida Caverns
Blackwater River
Pensacola
Big Lagoon
Tallahassee
Suwannee River
Little Talbot Island
Jacksonville
ATLANTIC OCEAN
Manatee Springs
Tomoka
Wekiwa Springs
Orlando
Gulf of Mexico
Caladesi Island
Tampa
Lake Kissimmee
Highlands Hammock
Jonathan Dickinson
Lake Okeechobee
Collier-Seminole
Miami
Everglades National Park
Fort Zachary Taylor
Key West
John Pennekamp Coral Reef

0   75   150 miles
0   75   150 kilometers

⊛ State capital
• Other city
■ State park

Map and Globe Skills

1. (Circle) the map title. What is this map about?

_____

_____

2. Place a check mark on the map legend. What does ■ mean?

_____

3. Draw the symbol for the state capital. _____

Kinds of Maps

Different kinds of maps show us different things. For example, look at the map below. It's a physical map of Florida. A physical map shows different land and water features, such as mountains, rivers, lakes, and oceans.

Now look at the map on the next page. This is a political map. A political map shows the borders of counties, states, countries, or other areas. This political map shows the 67 counties in Florida.

THINK · PAIR · SHARE
Think of a question to ask a partner about the maps on these pages. Then have your partner ask you a question. Check your answers with one another.

How are political and physical maps similar?

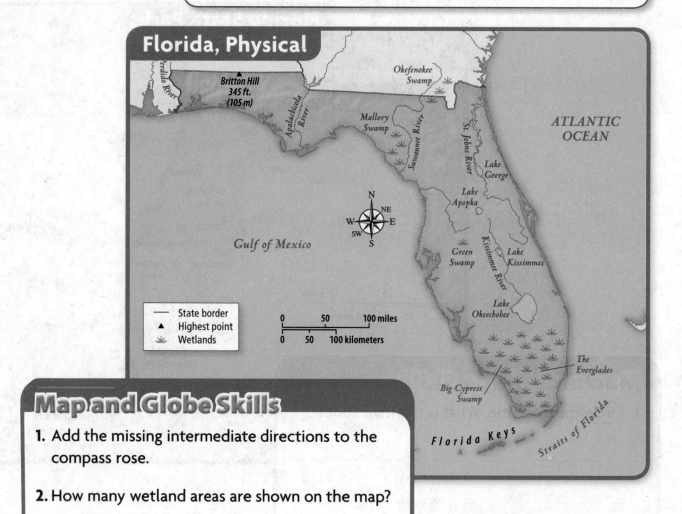

Florida, Physical

State border
▲ Highest point
☙ Wetlands

0   50   100 miles
0   50   100 kilometers

Map and Globe Skills

1. Add the missing intermediate directions to the compass rose.

2. How many wetland areas are shown on the map?

3. What direction is Lake Okeechobee from the St. Johns River?

NGSS Standards
SS.4.G.1.1 Identify physical features of Florida.
SS.4.G.1.4 Interpret political and physical maps using map elements (title, compass rose, cardinal directions, intermediate directions, symbols, legend, scale, longitude, latitude).

More Map Elements

You probably remember that the **cardinal directions** are north, south, east, and west. You probably also remember that the **intermediate directions** are halfway between any two cardinal directions. Northeast, northwest, southeast, and southwest are the four intermediate directions. Directions help us find places.

A **compass rose** is a symbol on a map that shows the cardinal and intermediate directions. A compass rose usually uses letters instead of words to **indicate** directions. For example, the letter E is used for east, and the letters NW are used for northwest.

During my travels, I've used a **map scale** many times. A map scale tells you the distance between places on a map. Here's how to use a map scale:

- Take a strip of paper and put it on the map between two places.

- Draw a mark where the first place is on the paper.

- Mark where the second place is on the paper.

- Place the strip of paper on the map scale. Put one of the marks at zero.

- Look at where the other mark is on the map scale. This tells you how far apart the two places are.

Map and Globe Skills

1. Add the missing cardinal directions to the compass rose.

2. Circle the county you live in on the map.

3. About how many miles apart are Jacksonville and Orlando?

_____

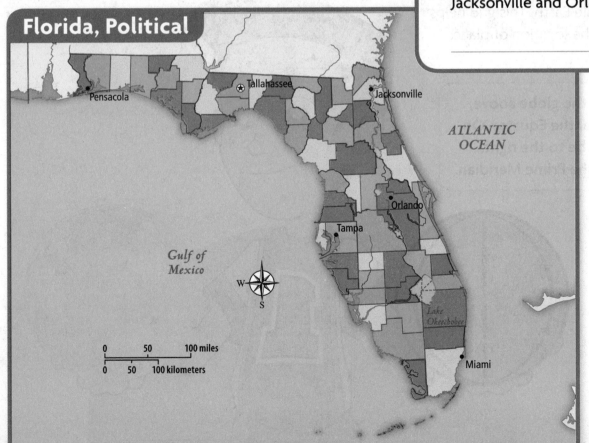

Florida, Political

Pensacola

Tallahassee

Jacksonville

ATLANTIC OCEAN

Orlando

Tampa

Gulf of Mexico

W—⊕—E
S

Lake Okeechobee

Miami

0   50   100 miles
0   50   100 kilometers

Latitude and Longitude

Have you noticed before that some maps and globes have lines on them? Some lines run east and west, while other lines run north and south. Lines that run north and south are called **latitude** lines. Latitude lines measure how far north or south a place is from the Equator. The Equator is an imaginary line that lies halfway between the North Pole and the South Pole. The lines of latitude north of the Equator are labeled N. Latitude lines south of the Equator are labeled S.

When you hold a basketball so that its lines run up and down, the lines look similar to **longitude** lines on a globe. Lines of longitude measure distance east or west of the Prime Meridian. The Prime Meridian is an imaginary line that goes around Earth from top to bottom. Lines of longitude east of the Prime Meridian are labeled E. Lines of longitude west of the Prime Meridian are labeled W.

Latitude and longitude are measured in degrees. The symbol for degrees looks like this: °. The Prime Meridian is at 0° longitude, and the Equator is at 0° latitude. Together, longitude and latitude lines create a grid over the whole Earth. This grid helps people find the location of places.

On the globe above, label the Equator. On the globe to the right, circle the Prime Meridian.

14

To give the location of a place, find the longitude and latitude lines that are closest to it. For instance, put your finger on Miami on the map below. Now find the latitude line (the lines that run north and south) that is closest to Miami. As you can see, Miami is nearest to the 26°N latitude line. Now find which longitude line (the lines that run east and west) is closest to Miami. Miami is at about 80°W longitude. So Miami is located at about 26°N, 80°W.

Map and Globe Skills

1. Find the latitude and longitude closest to Gainesville.

_____

2. What city is nearest to 28°N, 81°W?

_____

3. About how miles is it from Miami to Tampa? _____

4. What direction is Miami from Lake Okeechobee? _____

Pensacola • ☆ Tallahassee • Jacksonville
Apalachicola • Gainesville •
Gulf of Mexico ATLANTIC OCEAN
Orlando • Melbourne
Tampa •
St. Petersburg •
Lake Okeechobee
Miami •
Florida Keys
Key West • *Straits of Florida*

0   100   200 miles
0   100   200 kilometers

30°N 29°N 28°N 27°N 26°N

86°W 85°W 84°W 83°W 82°W 81°W 80°W 79°W 78°W

NGSS Standards
SS.4.G.1.2 Locate and label cultural features on a Florida map. **SS.4.G.1.4** Interpret political and physical maps using map elements (title, compass rose, cardinal directions, intermediate directions, symbols, legend, scale, longitude, latitude).

Lesson 1

? Essential Question How do maps help us understand places?

_____

_____

_____

Go back to *Show As You Go!* on pages 2–3.

networks
connected.mcgraw-hill.com
• Games • Assessment

Florida's Physical and Cultural Geography

(t1) Courtesy of the State Archives of Florida. (b) MediaImages / Punchstock

? Essential Question

What makes places unique and different?
What do you think?

_____

_____

_____

_____

Words To Know

Look at the words below. Rank them based on how much you know about them. Put a 1 next to the word you know the most about. Put a 6 next to the word you know the least about.

_____ **geography**

_____ ***affect**

_____ **strait**

_____ **region**

_____ **landform**

_____ **tourist**

NGSS Standards
SS.4.A.1.1 Analyze primary and secondary sources to identify significant individuals and events throughout Florida history.
SS.4.G.1.1 Identify the physical features of Florida.

In 1947 President Harry Truman spoke about a special place in Florida.

"Here is land . . . in its quiet beauty, serving not as the source of water, but as the last receiver of it. To its natural **abundance** we owe the spectacular plant and animal life that distinguishes this place from all others in our country."

abundance having a lot of something

What place in Florida do you think Truman was talking about?

Everglades

Check your prediction as you read this lesson.

In his speech, President Truman was describing part of Florida's **geography**. Geography is the study of Earth. Geography includes types of land, bodies of water, weather, plants, and animals in a place. It also includes what happens because of the activities of people on Earth. Geography is important because it **affects** your life. The type of food you eat, what you wear, and even the kind of home you live in are all influenced by geography.

Florida's Physical Geography

Florida is easy to find on a map. That's because Florida is a peninsula. A peninsula is a piece of land that is surrounded on three sides by water. What bodies of water are these? The Gulf of Mexico is on the west side, and the Atlantic Ocean is on the east side. To the south, the area of water between the Gulf of Mexico and the Atlantic Ocean is known as the **Straits** of Florida. A strait is a narrow passage of water between two larger bodies of water.

Florida is in the Southeast **region** of the United States. A region is an area with common features that make it different from other areas. The United States has four other regions—the Northeast, Midwest, Southwest, and West.

Each region has physical features, such as mountains and rivers, that define it. All states in the same region, such as the Southeast, share some physical features. For example, many states in the Southeast have areas called plains. Plains are large areas of land that are mostly flat. Most of the land in Florida is a plain.

A plain is a type of **landform**. Landforms are any of the shapes that make up Earth's surface. In addition to plains, Florida has other landforms. The state has gentle hills, lakes, rivers, and beaches.

> **Circle** the names of the three bodies of water that surround Florida.

> **NGSS Standards**
> **SS.4.G.1.1** Identify the physical features of Florida.

> **Underline** the landforms that Florida has.

The Southeast

PA
NJ
OH
DE
IN
MD
IL
WV
VA
KS
MO
KY
OK
TN
NC
AR
SC
MS
AL
GA
TX
LA
ATLANTIC OCEAN
FL
N
W E
S
Gulf of Mexico

0   200   400 miles
0   200   400 kilometers

Map and Globe Skills

1. How many states share a border with Florida?

_____

2. Color Florida orange. Color the states that border Florida blue.

3. How many states in the Southeast border the Atlantic Ocean?

_____

Florida's Regions and Landforms

NGSS Standards
SS.4.G.1.1 Identify the physical features of Florida.

Geographers—people who study geography—divide the state of Florida into three main regions: the Gulf Coastal Plain, the Central Highlands, and the Atlantic Coastal Plain.

Britton Hill
345 ft.
(105 m)

Gulf Coastal Plain

Where do you think you'll find the Gulf Coastal Plain? Along the Gulf of Mexico, of course! This lowland region is on the western side of the state. It extends from the western part of the panhandle all the way down to the southern tip of the state. The panhandle is the part of northern Florida that looks like the handle of a frying pan.

   Much of the Gulf Coastal Plain is flat grassland, though it also contains forests and wetland areas. Wetlands are low areas of land, such as swamps, that are partially covered with water. Forests line the northern part of the Plain in the panhandle. Along the western coast of Florida, the Plain also includes capes and barrier islands. Capes are pieces of land that stick out into the ocean. Barrier islands are small sandy islands that run alongside the coast.

N
W   E
S

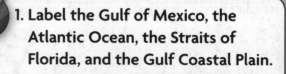

▲ The Gulf Coastal Plain has beautiful beaches.

1. Label the Gulf of Mexico, the Atlantic Ocean, the Straits of Florida, and the Gulf Coastal Plain.

2. Shade the Gulf Coastal Plain region blue.

18

Purestock/Getty Images

Central Highlands

The Central Highlands, which are sometimes called the Florida Uplands, are different from the lowland areas. Don't be fooled, though—just because the name says "highlands" doesn't mean the land is very high. The land here is just a little higher than the land in the Coastal Plains. Most of the Central Highlands lie in the central part of Florida. Lakes, gentle hills, and forests are found here. The panhandle also has some highlands. In fact, the highest point in Florida—Britton Hill—is found in the panhandle.

1. Color the Central Highlands red.
2. Label this region.
3. Circle Britton Hill on the map.

Forests and gentle hills cover the Central Highlands. ▶

Many birds and plants occupy Florida's wetlands. ▼

NGSS Standards
SS.4.G.1.1 Identify the physical features of Florida.

Atlantic Coastal Plain

As you can probably guess, the Atlantic Coastal Plain lies along the Atlantic Ocean. Just like the Gulf Coastal Plain, the Atlantic Coastal Plain has flat grasslands, forests, and wetlands. The Atlantic Coastal Plain isn't just in Florida. It runs for hundreds of miles along the coast of the Atlantic Ocean. The Plain also includes barrier islands, capes, and the Florida Keys. The Keys are a line of small islands off the southern coast of Florida. The largest island, Key Largo, is only about 30 miles long.

1. Color the Atlantic Coastal Plain green.
2. Label this region.
3. Label the Florida Keys.

19

Main Idea and Key
Details Remember that the main idea tells what a passage is about. Key details tell about the main idea.

Read the first paragraph on this page again. Circle the main idea and underline the key details.

DID YOU KNOW?
Florida's state song, "The Swanee River (Old Folks at Home)" by Stephen Foster, gets its name from the Suwannee River.

Florida's Water

Every region of Florida has important bodies of water. Our state is surrounded on three sides by salt water, and its interior has dozens of freshwater rivers and streams. Lakes—thousands of them—also dot the interior of Florida. Lake Okeechobee, the largest of these lakes, is one of the largest lakes in the nation. Florida also has many bays. A bay is a body of water that is partly surrounded by land.

Florida's rivers have been important to the state throughout its history. Rivers provide transportation and also provide water for growing plants. Two of Florida's northern rivers make up part of our state borders. The Perdido River on the western side of the panhandle is the border with Alabama. The Saint Marys River in the northeast marks the border with Georgia. The Saint Johns River, a major river in the state, runs through northern Florida too.

Some Florida rivers begin in other states. One of these rivers is the Apalachicola. It runs from Georgia through the Florida panhandle to the Gulf of Mexico. The Suwannee River also starts in Georgia and ends on Florida's northwestern coast.

NGSS Standards
SS.4.G.1.1 Identify the physical features of Florida. **SS.4.G.1.4** Interpret political and physical maps using map elements (title, compass rose, cardinal directions, intermediate directions, symbols, legend, scale, longitude, latitude).

Florida's Bodies of Water

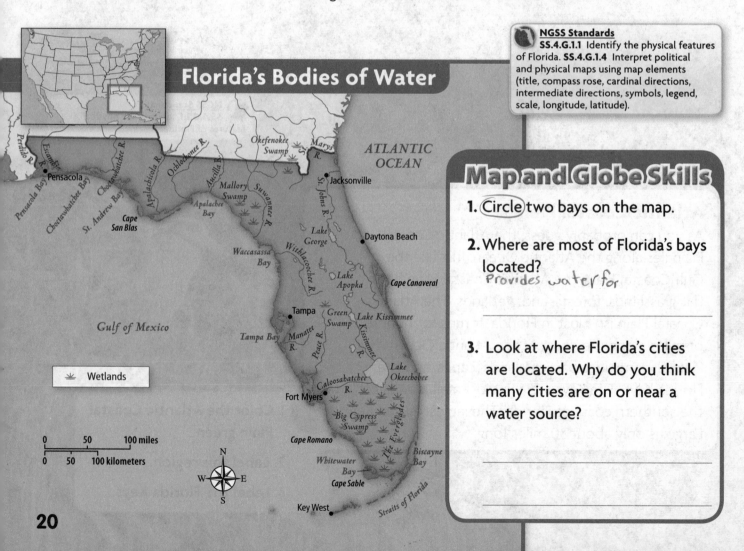

Wetlands

0   50   100 miles
0   50   100 kilometers

Map and Globe Skills

1. Circle two bays on the map.

2. Where are most of Florida's bays located?
Provides water for
_____

3. Look at where Florida's cities are located. Why do you think many cities are on or near a water source?
_____
_____

▲ The Everglades cover a large part of the southern tip of Florida.

Another important river in Florida is the Kissimmee. It flows through central Florida, draining many of the small lakes into Lake Okeechobee. This water then moves south through the Big Cypress Swamp and the Everglades. These two places are examples of wetlands.

NGSS Standards
SS.4.G.1.1 Identify the physical features of Florida.

Did you know that the Everglades is one of the most famous wetland areas in the United States? The Everglades is a chain of lakes, rivers, and wetlands that spread out over a large portion of southern Florida. The Everglades is home to more than 1,000 kinds of plants and numerous animals, including more than 350 kinds of birds. Other animals, such as the endangered American crocodile and the Florida panther, also make their home there.

A woman named Marjory Stoneman Douglas spent her life trying to protect the Everglades. She described the area as "one of the unique regions of the earth." In 1947 the government created Everglades National Park to protect the area. President Harry Truman gave a speech at the creation of the park.

The Key Deer is an endangered species. ▼

Fact or Opinion? *Everglades National Park is the best park in the country.*

_____

(t) Jupiterimages / Getty, (br) JTB Photo/age fotostock

21

Tourist Attractions and Cities

DID YOU KNOW?

Other tourist attractions in Florida include:

- Gulf Islands National Seashore near Pensacola
- Florida Museum of Natural History in Gainesville
- Great Explorations Children's Museum in St. Petersburg
- South Beach in Key West

Walt Disney World ▼

The Everglades is an example of one of the many **tourist** attractions in Florida. Tourists are people who travel for fun. Millions of tourists visit Florida's attractions every year. What tourist attractions do you know about?

Tourist attractions are located all over the state. Many of them are located in Florida's major cities. For example, Jacksonville is Florida's largest city with about 800,000 people. There, football fans like watching the Jacksonville Jaguars play. Another sport many people enjoy is racing. Many tourists visit Florida each February for the Daytona 500 car race in Daytona Beach.

Some tourist attractions in Florida focus on animals. Miami has a famous zoo called Zoo Miami. This zoo has no cages! Fences and ditches filled with water keep the animals separated from each other—and the visitors. In Tampa, visitors can view ocean life at the Florida Aquarium.

Florida is home to some popular theme parks. The most famous of these is Walt Disney World in Orlando. Orlando is also home to Sea World and Universal Studios. These theme parks attract more than 20 million visitors each year from around the world.

Our state has many other tourist attractions. For example, Kennedy Space Center in Cape Canaveral draws lots of visitors every year. Tourists also enjoy our state capital of Tallahassee. Members of our government work at the State Capitol building there.

Cape Canaveral ▼

NGSS Standards
SS.4.G.1.2 Locate and label cultural features on a Florida map.
SS.4.G.1.4 Interpret political and physical maps using map elements (title, compass rose, cardinal directions, intermediate directions, symbols, legend, scale, longitude, latitude).

Florida Cities and Tourist Attractions

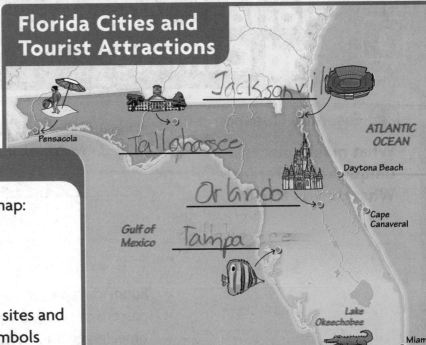

ATLANTIC OCEAN

Jacksonville

Pensacola

Tallahassee

Daytona Beach

Orlando

Cape Canaveral

Gulf of Mexico

Tampa

Lake Okeechobee

Miami

The Everglades

Key West

Straits of Florida

Map and Globe Skills

1. Label the following cities on the map:
   - Orlando
   - Tallahassee
   - Tampa
   - Jacksonville
2. Create a symbol for the following sites and put them on the map. Add the symbols and their labels to the map legend below.
   - Zoo Miami
   - Kennedy Space Center
   - Daytona 500 car race

 State Capitol

 Jacksonville Jaguars Stadium

The Everglades

 Gulf Islands National Seashore

Florida Aquarium

South Beach

Walt Disney World

Lesson 2

(?) Essential Question   What makes places unique and different?

_____

_____

_____

Go back to *Show As You Go!* on pages 2–3. ◀◀◀

(?) Essential Question

**What makes places unique and different?
What do you think?**

_____

_____

_____

_____

_____

Words To Know

Look at the words below. Circle the words you already know. Put a question mark next to the words that you don't know.

climate

precipitation

*develop

drought

hurricane

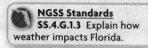

NGSS Standards
SS.4.G.1.3 Explain how weather impacts Florida.

24

*Did you know that Florida is called the "Sunshine State"?
Why do you think it has this nickname?*

_____

_____

Sunny days are one part of Florida's **climate**. Climate is the pattern of weather in a certain place over a long period of time. In general, Florida has a warm, mild climate. One reason for Florida's warm climate is its location on Earth. Florida is closer to the Equator than any other state, except for Hawaii. The closer a place is to the Equator, the warmer it is. Elevation also affects temperatures. Elevation is how high an area is. The lower an area's elevation, the warmer its temperature. Florida is a very low-lying state, and so it has warm temperatures.

Florida's warm, mild climate has a big impact on the state. Warm temperatures and lots of rain helps farmers grow crops. It even stays warm enough in some places in Florida that crops can be grown in winter. The state's warm weather also makes it a popular destination for tourists.

You're never more than 60 miles from a beach in any part of Florida. ▼

(bkgd) Bloomimage/Corbis, (b) John Coletti / Getty Images

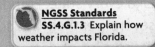
Look at the chart below. As you can see, the temperatures stay warm throughout the year in Florida. Warm weather year round isn't always a good thing, however. Florida summers can be very hot and humid. *Humid* refers to how much moisture is in the air. When the weather is humid, the air feels even warmer than the actual temperature. Many people who live in Florida during the winter leave in the humid summer to escape the weather.

In addition to temperatures, climate also includes the kind of **precipitation** a place gets. Precipitation is any water, such as rain, sleet, snow, or hail, that falls to Earth. Most of Florida gets 50 to 60 inches of rain per year, making it one of the wettest states in the Southeast. Florida almost never gets snow, however. In fact, snow falls so rarely in Florida that some people in our state have never even seen snow except on television!

NGSS Standards
SS.4.G.1.3 Explain how weather impacts Florida.

DID YOU KNOW?
In 1977 light snow fell in Miami. This was the first time in its recorded history that Miami has received snow.

How does Florida's mild climate impact our state?

_____

_____

_____

THINK · PAIR · SHARE
With a partner, **develop** a list of as many different kinds of weather as you can.

Chart and Graph Skills

Interpret a Chart

1. **Which city has the lowest average temperature in January?**

   Tallahssee

2. **Which city has an average temperature of 83°F in July?**

   Miami

3. **Which city has the highest temperature difference between January and July?**

   Key West

Average Temperatures		
City	**January**	**July**
Tampa	61°F	82°F
Jacksonville	53°F	82°F
Miami	68°F	83°F
Orlando	61°F	82°F
Tallahassee	52°F	82°F
Key West	70°F	84°F

Source: NOAA National Weather Service

25

Severe Weather

Like every state, Florida can experience severe weather. This severe weather can cause a lot of damage and problems.

NGSS Standards
SS.4.G.1.3 Explain how weather impacts Florida.

▼ **Droughts can kill crops.**

Drought

Usually, Florida gets plenty of rain. Sometimes, however, there is a **drought**—a long period without rain. Droughts are dangerous to crops, animals, and people. If a drought lasts long enough, crops and animals might die, which hurts the farming business. During a drought, local governments may limit the amount of water that people can use. For example, people might not be allowed to water their yards and gardens for awhile.

Underline the definition of drought.

Thunderstorms

Thunderstorms are dangerous for a few reasons. They can bring too much rain and can result in flooding. A flood happens when a body of water overflows its banks. Thunderstorms also produce lightning. Lightning strikes can hurt people and start fires. Thunderstorms are also dangerous because of the high winds they can bring. High winds can knock down trees and cause damage to buildings.

Lightning strikes are dangerous. ▶

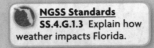
NGSS Standards
SS.4.G.1.3 Explain how weather impacts Florida.

Hurricanes

Hurricanes are severe storms that bring heavy rainfall and very strong winds. At wind speeds starting at 74 miles an hour, mild hurricanes usually don't hurt buildings. But the very worst hurricanes can have wind speeds over 150 miles an hour. That's strong enough to rip roofs right off of buildings! Some houses might be blown over completely. Hurricane winds often cause storm surges. Storm surges are huge ocean waves. These waves, whipped up by the strong winds, can flood coastal areas, causing major destruction of property. Hurricanes not only cause property damage, but they can also harm people.

▲ Hurricanes can cause widespread devastation.

Fill in the boxes below with the impact each type of severe weather has on Florida.

drought ⟹	
thunderstorm ⟹	
hurricane ⟹	

Lesson **3**

 Essential Question What makes places unique and different?

_____

_____

_____

_____

Go back to *Show As You Go!* on pages 2–3. ⟪

 **netw⊙rks**   **There's More Online!**
● Games ● Assessment

? Essential Question

How does location affect culture?

What do you think?

_____

_____

_____

_____

Words To Know

Pick a symbol to draw next to each word to show how much you know about what the word means.

? = I have no idea!
▲ = I know a little.
★ = I know a lot.

_____ culture

_____ *vary

_____ palisade

_____ midden

_____ fertile

The geography and environment of Florida that you have learned about in this unit greatly affected the first people who lived in the area. These people are called Native Americans.

Florida's first Native Americans lived thousands of years ago. Life was very different back then. At this time, stores, cars, and electricity didn't exist. Think about how you would have survived long ago. How would you have gotten food? Clothes? Shelter?

hunting, farming, fishing, make there on shelter, dead animal skin

_____

_____

To survive long ago, you would have used things from the environment, just like the Native Americans did. Their environment provided most of the things they needed. They ate animals and plants that lived and grew near their homes. They also made their clothes from these animals and plants. Native Americans built homes and other buildings from trees and other plants. They also created tools, such as weapons and utensils, from things they found in their environment.

▼ Native Americans ate animals that lived in their environment.

Florida Tribes

Do you know the names of any Native American tribes that lived in Florida? These tribes included the Apalachee, the Timucua, the Tocobaga, the Calusa, and the Tequesta. Find where each tribe lived in Florida on the map below.

Tribes in Florida had similarities and differences. As you just read, each tribe relied upon their environment for food, clothing, and shelter. In fact, these different tribes ate many of the same kinds of foods. They also had similar types of clothing and homes.

However, each tribe in Florida had its own **culture**. Culture is the way of life of a group of people. Culture includes people's homes, clothing, food, and artwork. The environment where each tribe lived affected their culture. For example, the tribes that lived along the coasts of Florida were good sailors. Tribes in northern Florida were farmers because the soil there was good for growing crops.

> **DID YOU KNOW?**
> Long ago, Native Americans lived all over the United States. These different tribes all depended on their environment for survival too.

NGSS Standards
SS.4.A.2.1 Compare Native American tribes of Florida.
SS.4.G.1.4 Interpret political and physical maps using map elements (title, compass rose, cardinal directions, intermediate directions, symbols, legend, scale, longitude, latitude).

Underline one similarity shared by the Native American tribes of Florida.

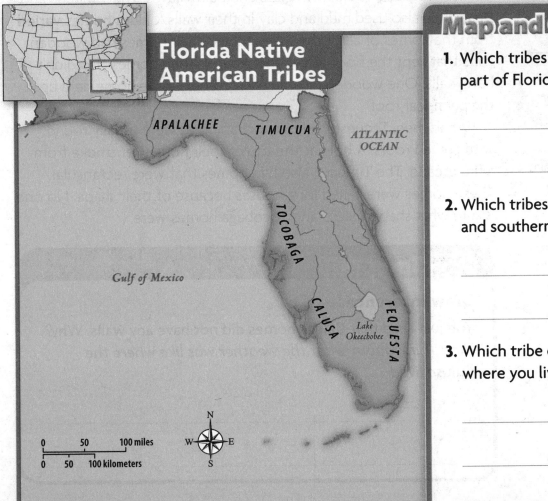

Florida Native American Tribes

APALACHEE TIMUCUA ATLANTIC OCEAN

TOCOBAGA

Gulf of Mexico

CALUSA TEQUESTA

Lake Okeechobee

0 50 100 miles
0 50 100 kilometers

Map and Globe Skills

1. Which tribes lived in the northern part of Florida?

_____

_____

2. Which tribes lived in the central and southern parts of Florida?

_____

_____

3. Which tribe or tribes lived near where you live today?

_____

_____

▲ A Timucua village

Homes and Villages

As you read this page, underline the materials that the Native Americans of Florida used to build their homes.

NGSS Standards
SS.4.A.2.1 Compare Native American tribes in Florida.

FUN FACTS
The Appalachian Mountains were named after the Apalachee.

The homes of the Native American tribes of Florida had similarities. All five tribes used wooden poles and branches for the frames of their homes. The Apalachee, Tequesta, Tocobaga, and Timucua all created walls and roofs from grass and palm leaves. The Timucua and Apalachee also used mud and clay in their walls. Calusa homes **varied** from the homes of all of the other tribes. Their homes had wooden stilts that kept the floor above the ground. Their homes also didn't have walls! One wooden pillar in each corner of the home held up the palm-leaf roof.

Apalachee, Tequesta, and Timucua homes were usually round with curved roofs. A hole at the top of their homes let smoke from a fire escape. The Timucua also had homes that were rectangular. These homes were called long houses because of their shape. No one is sure what shape Calusa and Tocobaga homes were.

Courtesy of the State Archives of Florida

Reading Skill

Draw Inferences

You just read that Calusa homes did not have any walls. Why? *Hint: Think about what the weather was like where the Calusa lived.*

_____

_____

The Native Americans of Florida lived in villages of many families. The Timucua, Apalachee, and Tocobaga arranged their homes around a central plaza, or open area. These plazas were gathering places for the tribes. The Timucua would also build a **palisade**, or a high wooden fence, around their villages. The palisade provided protection for the village. Apalachee and Timucua villages also had buildings that stored extra food.

If you could have visited a Tocobaga, Tequesta, or Calusa village, you would have seen something interesting—mounds. These mounds were **middens**, or trash piles of shells, bones, and other items. The Tocobaga and Calusa built many of their buildings on top of these mounds. The Calusa even created an entire island called Mound Key from discarded shells.

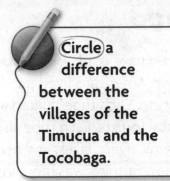

(Circle) a difference between the villages of the Timucua and the Tocobaga.

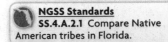
NGSS Standards
SS.4.A.2.1 Compare Native American tribes in Florida.

Choose two tribes and compare and contrast their homes and villages. Fill in the chart below.

Similarities	Differences

▼ A Calusa village

31

Food

As you have read, the environment where Native Americans lived provided the food they ate. Each tribe hunted and gathered in nearby forests. Each tribe also fished in the streams, rivers, lakes, and oceans near their homes. Farming was more important to some tribes than to others.

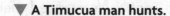
▼ A Timucua man hunts.

Hunting

Each tribe in Florida hunted for food. Some of the animals they ate included deer, bear, turkey, and other forest animals. Have you ever had alligator for dinner? The Timucua and the Tequesta often ate this reptile.

The men in each tribe did the hunting. Different tools helped them. The Timucua used bows, arrows, and spears when they hunted. The Tocobaga and the Calusa used a throwing stick called an *atlatl* to hunt.

> **What tools did the Timucua use to hunt?**
> _____

▲ Atlatl

Gathering

Gathering food to eat was important to each tribe in Florida too. Women and girls did the gathering. They collected fruits, nuts, and berries that grew naturally in their surroundings. In southern Florida, the Calusa and the Tequesta both gathered a fruit called sea grapes. The Calusa also ate papaya and prickly pear fruit. The Tequesta enjoyed coco plums and hog plums.

> **True or False?** *All Florida tribes gathered food.*
> _____

▲ Sea grapes

NGSS Standards
SS.4.A.2.1 Compare Native American tribes in Florida.

Farming

The Apalachee did more farming than any other Native American tribe in Florida. They farmed because the soil where they lived was **fertile**, or good for growing plants. Apalachee women grew corn, beans, squash, and other vegetables.

Timucua and Tocobaga women also did some farming. They grew the same kinds of vegetables that the Apalachee did. The Calusa and the Tequesta did little farming. The land where they lived was sandy and not very fertile. They got plenty of food from the fishing they did.

 Put a box around the names of the tribes that did not farm very much.

▲ Apalachee women farming

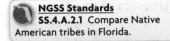 **NGSS Standards**
SS.4.A.2.1 Compare Native American tribes in Florida.

Fishing

Fishing was important to each tribe, especially the ones that lived in southern Florida. Both women and men fished. Near shorelines, women collected shellfish, such as crabs, oysters, and clams. Men used nets, traps, and spears to catch mullet, catfish, and many other kinds of fish. The Calusa and the Tocobaga even caught manatee!

Canoes helped men fish along the waterways of Florida. The tribes used tools made from stones and shells to scrape out the insides of tree logs to make the canoes.

Underline the kinds of fish that people ate.

Calusa fishing ▼

▲ An Apalachee family at their home

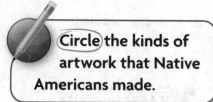

Circle the kinds of artwork that Native Americans made.

More Parts of Culture

The cultures of the five Native American tribes of Florida had other similarities and differences. For example, each tribe wore the same kinds of clothing. Men wore deerskin clothes, and women wore clothes that were woven from Spanish moss and other plants. When it got cool in winter, the Apalachee wore capes and cloaks made from animal furs to stay warm.

Artwork was important to these Native American tribes. Women from all of the tribes made pottery, usually from clay. Some of this pottery had designs on it. Pottery was used for cooking and for storing things. The Timucua and the Calusa made and wore jewelry too. The Calusa used shells, shark teeth, and other animal bones in their jewelry. They also made masks to wear for special events.

Trading helped each tribe get the things they needed and wanted. All of the tribes traded with others for things that they could not find in their environment. Native Americans walked or used canoes to travel to other villages to trade.

Calusa artwork ▼

NGSS Standards
SS.4.A.1.1 Analyze primary and secondary resources to identify significant individuals and events in Florida history.
SS.4.A.2.1 Compare Native American tribes of Florida.

THINK • PAIR • SHARE
Think about what each of the artifacts shown here was made of and how each was probably used. Share your ideas with a partner.

Calusa artifacts ▼

▲ Canoe

34

(l) MPI/Getty Images, (c) Courtesy of the State Archives of Florida, (r) Tim Chapman/Newscom

Comparing Tribes

Choose two Native American tribes from this lesson.
Write their names on the lines in the Venn diagram.
Compare and contrast them below.

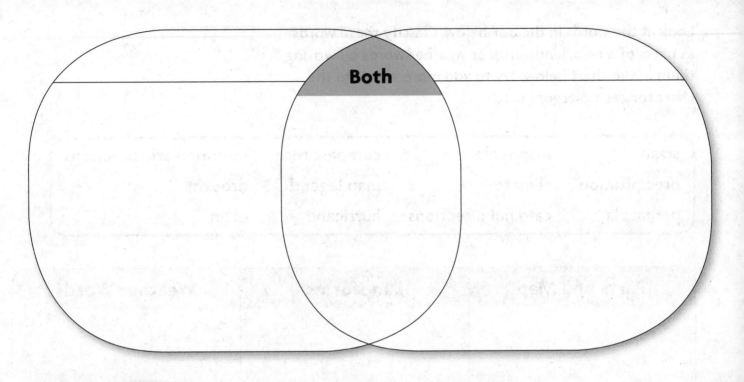

Both

Lesson **4**

 Essential Question How does location affect culture?

_____

_____

_____

_____

_____

Go back to _Show As You Go!_ on pages 2–3.

 netw rks

There's More Online!
● Games ● Assessment

35

networks **There's More Online!**
● Games ● Assessment

StockTrek/Getty Images

Look at the words in the box below. Classify these words as parts of a map, landforms, or weather words by writing them in the chart below. Try to add more words to the chart for each category too.

strait	map scale	compass rose	intermediate directions
precipitation	climate	map legend	drought
peninsula	cardinal directions	hurricane	plain

Parts of a Map	Landforms	Weather Words

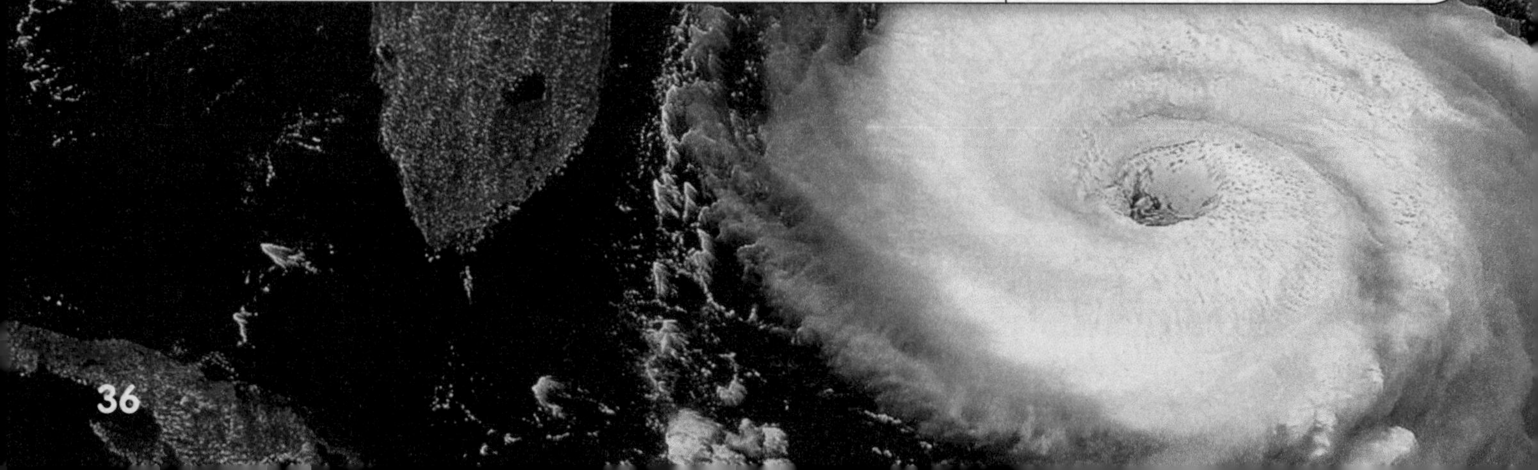

Unit Project

Imagine that a local tourism company has hired you to create the design for a 3-D, salt dough map of Florida. They are going to display it in their lobby to greet their customers. Think about what your map will look like. Before you begin making your design, look back at **Show As You Go!** on pages 2 and 3 to review your notes. Read the list below to see what should be included in your design. As you work, check off each task.

Your design should...   **Yes, it does!**

have a title, compass rose, and map legend.   ☐

show Florida's regions, landforms, and bodies of water.   ☐

label major bodies of water.   ☐

label the capital and at least five other major cities.   ☐

label five tourist attractions.   ☐

use two print or electronic media sources as references.   ☐

> **NGSS Standards**
> **SS.4.A.1.2** Synthesize information related to Florida history through print and electronic media.

Think about the Big Idea

BIG IDEA 💡 Location affects how people live.

What did you learn in this unit that helps you understand the Big Idea?

_____

_____

_____

_____

Read the passage "Lake Okeechobee" and then answer Numbers 1 and 2.

Lake Okeechobee

1　LAKE Okeechobee is one of Florida's greatest treasures. It is located in the southeastern part of the state. The Everglades borders it on the south. The Kissimmee River drains into the lake on the north side. The lake is the state's largest one, and its name reflects this.

2　"Okeechobee" is a Native American word that means "big water." The lake is about 35 miles long and 30 miles wide. This size makes it one of the biggest lakes in the United States. In fact, the Lake Okeechobee is so large that it can be seen from space!

3　The lake provides great recreational opportunities for tourists. People can enjoy picnics and campfires at many camp sites that surround the lake. The Lake Okeechobee Scenic Trail is a hiking and bicycle path that goes all the way around the lake. That makes the trail 110 miles all together!

4　People can also go on boat rides and view a variety of wildlife on the lake. They might see alligators, blue herons and other birds, and turtles. Lake Okeechobee might be best known, however, for its fishing. Bass fishing is very popular in the lake's waters.

"Lake Okeechobee" property of McGraw-Hill Education.

GO ON →

Now answer Numbers 1 and 2. Base your answers on the passage "Lake Okeechobee."

1 This question has two parts. First, answer Part A. Then, answer Part B.

Part A What is the main idea of this passage?

Ⓐ Lake Okeechobee can be seen from space.

Ⓑ Lake Okeechobee has a walking trail around it.

Ⓒ Lake Okeechobee is popular with people who fish.

Ⓓ Lake Okeechobee is an important part of Florida.

Part B Which sentence from the passage supports your answer in Part A?

Ⓐ "Lake Okeechobee is one of Florida's greatest treasures."

Ⓑ "The lake is the state's largest one, and its name reflects this."

Ⓒ "The lake provides great recreational opportunities for tourists."

Ⓓ "Lake Okeechobee might be best known, however, for its fishing."

2 Where did Lake Okeechobee get its name from?

Ⓐ a Native American word

Ⓑ a tourist who visited the lake

Ⓒ a type of boat that travels on the lake

Ⓓ a vote that the people of Florida took

GO ONLINE to connected.mcgraw-hill.com for enhanced Florida Test Preparation options, available through Engrade.

Exploration and Colonization of Florida

BIG IDEA People's actions affect others.

Hundreds of years ago, Europeans began arriving on the shores of Florida. Why did they come here? What did they find? In this unit, you will read about why Europeans came to Florida. You will also read about the Native Americans who already lived there and what happened when these different cultures met. As you read, think about how the actions of the different groups of people from Europe affected Native Americans—and each other.

There's More Online!
- Skill Builders
- Vocabulary Flashcards

Show As You Go! After you read each lesson in this unit, use these pages to record important information that you learned about each topic. You will use your notes to help you complete a project at the end of the unit.

Fold page here.

Challenges of Exploration

_____

_____

_____

_____

Motivations for and Causes of Exploration

_____

_____

_____

_____

_____

Important Communities

_____

_____

_____

_____

Effects of Exploration

_____

_____

_____

_____

_____

Reading Skill

NGSS Standards
LAFS.4.RI.1.3 Explain events, procedures, ideas, or concepts in a historical, scientific, or technical text, including what happened and why, based on specific information in the text.

Understand Cause and Effect

When you drop a book, what happens? It falls to the floor, right? This is an example of a cause and an effect. Dropping the book is the cause. A cause is an action or event that makes something else happen. The book falling to the floor is an effect. An effect is what happens because of a cause. Figuring out causes and effects will help you understand what you read.

LEARN IT

To find causes and effects:

- **Ask yourself, "What happened?" This will be the effect.**

- **Ask yourself, "Why did that happen?" This will be the cause.**

- **Look for the clue words *because*, *so*, and *as a result*. These words often point to causes and effects.**

> **Effect**
> This sentence tells what happened.

> **Clue Word**

> **Cause**
> This section tells why the effect happened.

In the 1400s, Europe and Asia were important trading partners. Many people became very rich from this trade. This is because Asia had goods that Europeans were willing to pay a lot of money for.

The trading route that connected Europe and Asia was dangerous and long. The whole journey could take years to complete. Europeans started to look for another way—a water route—to Asia.

▼ Travelers along the Silk Road

The Mukashi Collection/Superstock/Getty Images

42

TRY IT

The graphic organizer below can help you keep track of causes and effects.
Fill it in with causes and effects from the paragraphs on page 42.

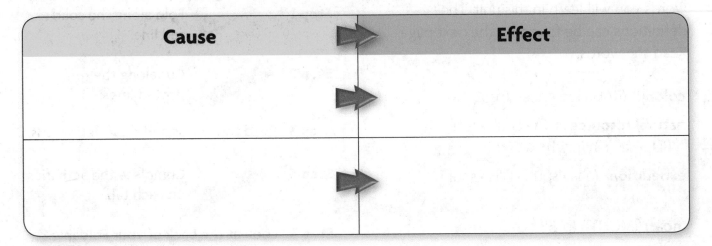

Cause		Effect

APPLY IT

- Review the steps for understanding cause and effect in Learn It.
- Read the passage below. Circle one cause. Underline its effect.
- Find another cause and circle it. Then underline its effect.

Juan Ponce de León was the first European to explore Florida. According to legend, one reason he explored Florida was that he heard stories about a magical fountain there. Drinking water from this fountain was supposed to make a person young again. In 1513 Ponce de León landed near what is today called Cape Canaveral. He and his men explored many places in Florida. They never found the so-called "Fountain of Youth."

Ponce de León (right) searching for the Fountain of Youth ▼

43

NGSS Standards
LAFS.4.RI.2.4 Determine the meaning of general academic and domain-specific words or phrases in a text relevant to a grade 4 topic or subject area.

The list below shows some important words you will learn in this unit. Their definitions can be found on the next page. Read the words.

colony (KAH • luh • nee) (p. 51)

natural resource (NA • chuh • ruhl REE • sawrs) (p. 51)

expedition (ehk • spuh • DIH • shuhn) (p. 53)

moat (MOHT) (p. 58)

militia (muh • LIH • shuh) (p. 60)

mission (MIH • shuhn) (p. 62)

treaty (TREE • tee) (p. 70)

agriculture (A • grih • kuhl • chuhr) (p. 73)

The **Foldable** on the next page will help you learn these important words. Follow the steps below to make your Foldable.

Step 1 Fold along the solid red line.

Step 2 Cut along the dotted lines.

Step 3 Read the words and their definitions.

Step 4 Complete the activities on each tab.

Step 5 Look at the back of your Foldable. Choose ONE of these activities for each word to help you remember its meaning:

- Draw a picture of the word.
- Write a description of the word.
- Write how the word is related to something you know.

▼ A mission in Florida

▲ An early colony in Florida

	FOLD Write the plural of the word *colony*.
A **colony** is a place that is ruled by another country.	
A **natural resource** is a material that comes from Earth.	Write a sentence using the words *natural resource*.
An **expedition** is a journey for a special purpose.	Write a synonym for the word *expedition*.
A **moat** is a ditch filled with water that surrounds a fort.	What do you think the purpose of a moat was?
A **militia** is a military unit.	Circle the words that belong with the word *militia*. soldiers fight army defend cow crop
A **mission** was a settlement where religion was taught.	Find two key words in the definition of mission. Write the words on the lines. _____ _____
A **treaty** is an agreement among countries.	Write an antonym for the word *treaty*.
Agriculture is the farming of crops and the raising of animals.	Cross out the word that does NOT belong with agriculture. food factory cattle soil barn farmer

colony	colony
natural resource	natural resource
expedition	expedition
moat	moat
militia	militia
mission	mission
treaty	treaty
agriculture	agriculture

CUT HERE

46

Primary Sources

NGSS Standards
SS.4.A.1.1 Analyze primary and secondary sources to identify significant individuals and events throughout Florida history.

Artifacts

Artifacts are an important type of primary source. Artifacts are objects made or used by people who lived in the past. Pottery, tools, and artwork are all types of artifacts. Artifacts give us clues about how people lived a long time ago.

In this unit, you'll learn about the European explorers who came to Florida. Artifacts from their journeys give us information about how they lived. To analyze an artifact, first describe what it looks like. What size, shape, and color is it? What is it made of? Then think about how the artifact might have been used. The answers to these questions will help you figure out how people who used the artifact might have lived.

© National Geographic Image Collection / Alamy

 Document-Based Questions

Study the artifacts above. Then complete the following activities.

- **Describe the artifacts.**

_____

_____

_____

- **What do you think they were used for?**

_____

_____

_____

Spanish Explorers in Florida

? Essential Question

Why do people explore?
What do you think?

_____

_____

_____

Words To Know

Write a number on each line to show how much you know about the meaning of each word.

1 = I have no idea!
2 = I know a little.
3 = I know a lot.

____ **conquistador**

____ ***motivation**

____ **colony**

____ ***rule**

____ **natural resource**

____ **expedition**

____ **slavery**

NGSS Standards
SS.4.A.3.1 Identify explorers who came to Florida and the motivations for their expeditions.
SS.4.G.1.4 Interpret political and physical maps using map elements (title, compass rose, cardinal directions, intermediate directions, symbols, legend, scale, longitude, latitude).

Do you know the end of this rhyme? Fill it in.

In fourteen hundred ninety-two, Columbus _____

_____ .

Check your answer at the bottom of the page.

It's true! In 1492, a man named Christopher Columbus sailed west from Europe. He hoped to find a new way to reach the continent of Asia. Instead, he landed on an island in the Bahamas, which is part of North America. His journey opened the door for other explorers to travel to North America. Some of them arrived in our state—Florida!

In fourteen hundred ninety-two, Columbus sailed the ocean blue.

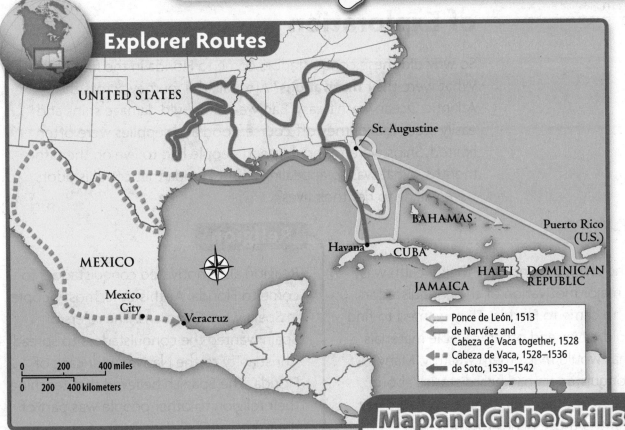

Explorer Routes

UNITED STATES

St. Augustine

BAHAMAS

Havana CUBA

Puerto Rico (U.S.)

HAITI DOMINICAN REPUBLIC

MEXICO

JAMAICA

Mexico City

Veracruz

| 0 | 200 | 400 miles |
| 0 | 200 | 400 kilometers |

← Ponce de León, 1513
← de Narváez and Cabeza de Vaca together, 1528
← Cabeza de Vaca, 1528–1536
← de Soto, 1539–1542

First Explorers

Who were these first explorers to come to Florida? They were called **conquistadors**. Conquistadors were explorers from the European country of Spain. They started arriving in North America in the 1500s. Juan Ponce de León was the first conquistador to arrive in Florida. He came in 1513. You can see his route on the map above. The map also shows the journeys taken by other conquistadors in Florida. Look back at this map as you read more about the journeys of the conquistadors in this lesson.

Map and Globe Skills

1. Label the cardinal directions on the compass rose.

2. Label the Atlantic Ocean and the Gulf of Mexico.

3. Who explored the east coast of Florida? In what year?

_____

4. Who explored the coastline of Florida's panhandle? In what year?

_____

DID YOU KNOW?
Conquistadors also explored Mexico and lands in the Caribbean.

49

NGSS Standards
SS.4.A.3.1 Identify explorers who came to Florida and the motivations for their expeditions.

Motivations for and Causes of Exploration

So why did these conquistadors come to Florida in the first place? What were their **motivations**? After all, the journey across the Atlantic Ocean wasn't easy. Bad weather could damage ships and easily steer the journey off course. Food and supplies were often limited. Ships weren't very big, and people had to live on them for months. What was *so* appealing about Florida that conquistadors were willing to risk their lives?

Gold

The chance to increase their wealth was a major motivation of the conquistadors who came to Florida. They wanted to find gold, silver, and other valuable materials that would make them wealthy. Many conquistadors had heard stories about the riches that North America had. They wanted those riches for themselves.

Religion

Religion also motivated conquistadors to come to Florida. At this time, most people in Spain were Christians. The rulers of Spain wanted the conquistadors to spread Christianity to the Native Americans of Florida. The Spanish believed that teaching their religion to other people was part of their duty as Christians.

DID YOU KNOW?

Before they came to Florida, the Spanish had already found gold. They found it on an island called Puerto Rico in the Caribbean.

The Spanish built churches that looked similar to this one to teach Christianity to Native Americans. ▼

(bkgd) Stockbyte/Getty Images, (b) eMcGraw-Hill Education

Colonies

Conquistadors also wanted to set up **colonies** in Florida. A colony is a place that is **ruled** by another country. Spain started colonies because of the benefits these colonies brought. For instance, having colonies meant that Spain controlled more land. The more land Spain controlled, the more power it had.

Colonies were also a source of wealth for Spain. Much of this wealth came from trade and **natural resources**. Natural resources are materials that come from Earth. Florida had many valuable natural resources, including wood, animals, and many kinds of plants and crops. Spain traded these resources and the products made from them with other countries. This trade earned Spain money. Having more wealth also increased the amount of power Spain had.

▲ Many natural resources from Florida were shipped back to Spain.

Keep in mind that before the 1500s, the Native Americans that you learned about in the last unit had Florida to themselves. The arrival of the conquistadors had major effects on them. Some effects were good—others were not. Native Americans learned about the foods, animals, and culture of the Europeans. Native Americans also gained new trading partners in the Europeans. However, Europeans also brought diseases that killed thousands of Native Americans. Fights with Europeans killed many Native Americans too. You'll learn more about these effects later in this unit.

Underline the effects of the arrival of Europeans on Native Americans.

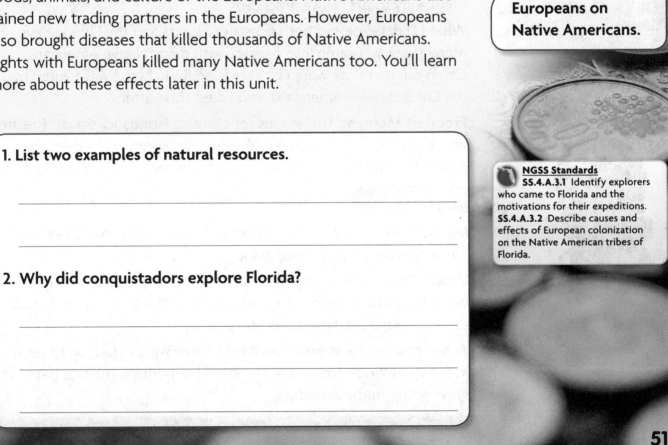

1. List two examples of natural resources.

_____

_____

2. Why did conquistadors explore Florida?

_____

_____

NGSS Standards
SS.4.A.3.1 Identify explorers who came to Florida and the motivations for their expeditions.
SS.4.A.3.2 Describe causes and effects of European colonization on the Native American tribes of Florida.

NGSS Standards
SS.4.A.3.1 Identify explorers who came to Florida and the motivations for their expeditions.

Florida Explorers

Exploring a new place isn't easy, as the conquistadors quickly learned. They faced a lot of challenges on their journeys, including trouble getting along with the Native Americans. These first journeys were mostly failures. The conquistadors didn't find riches, and the colonies they tried to set up didn't last. Few, if any, Native Americans learned about Christianity. Below, read about some of these conquistadors who came to Florida.

As you read about each conquistador, circle the places that he explored.

1513

Juan Ponce de León

Motivations: Many people think that I came to Florida in 1513 to find the Fountain of Youth. This magical fountain was supposed to make a person become young again. But I really came because I wanted to explore new areas and find gold. I also enslaved Native Americans. On my second trip to Florida, I tried to start a colony and spread Christianity to the Native Americans.

What I Did: I explored both coasts of Florida and the Florida Keys. Along the way, I came into contact with many Native Americans. Often our meetings were not very friendly. In fact, I was injured by the Calusa Native Americans, and I died soon after.

Proudest Moment: I'm famous for claiming Florida for Spain. The area where I landed was covered with plants in bloom, so I gave it the name *Florida*. This means "the land of flowers."

FUN FACTS
A woman named Juana Ruiz was part of Ponce de León's first voyage. She might have been the first European woman in North America!

Juan Garrido

Motivations: I was a conquistador, so I wanted to explore new areas and earn riches. Sadly, I died poor.

What I Did: I was born in Africa and spent time in Europe. After I came to North America, I explored Florida with Juan Ponce de León. Later on in my life, I explored Mexico.

Achievements: I was probably the first free African person to set foot in North America. I'm also remembered as perhaps the first person to grow wheat in the Americas.

1528

Pánfilo de Narváez

Motivations: When I arrived in Florida in 1528, I wanted to start a colony and find gold. I was disappointed when the colony didn't work out. I also didn't find any gold. But I did explore the western coast and panhandle of Florida.

What I Did: I had some big problems during my **expedition**. (In case you didn't know, an expedition is a journey for a special purpose.) I split my group into two—a land force and a water force. Each was supposed to explore and then reconnect. But things didn't work out that way. I was leading the land force, and we got stranded. We tried to sail to Mexico, but a storm hit us. Many were killed, including me.

Álvar Núñez Cabeza de Vaca

Motivations: I was part of Pánfilo de Narváez's expedition to Florida. I wanted to help him find gold and start a colony.

What I Did: I was lucky because I survived the storm that took so many lives. Some other people also made it through the storm, and this group kept trying to get to Mexico. Only four of us finally made it there, though. Along the way, we explored much of the southwest part of North America and learned about the Native Americans who lived there. My report of our journey was later published in Spain.

Quote: "The country is mostly flat, the soil sandy and firm. Throughout it there are many large trees and open woodlands . . . There are many large and small lakes . . ."

NGSS Standards
SS.4.A.3.1 Identify explorers who came to Florida and the motivations for their expeditions.

Estéban Dorantes

What I Did: I was born in Africa and lived in Spain for awhile. I was sold into **slavery**. Slavery is the practice of treating people as property and forcing them to work. So I came to Florida as an enslaved person in de Narváez's expedition. I was one of the four men from that expedition who eventually made it to Mexico. Toward the end of my life, I explored Mexico and parts of southwest North America.

Other Names: Estebanico, Estevanico, Estéban de Dorantes

Write one similarity among these explorers.

_____

_____

NGSS Standards
SS.4.A.3.1 Identify explorers who came to Florida and the motivations for their expeditions.
SS.4.A.9.1 Utilize timelines to sequence key events in Florida history.

(bkgd) Brand X Pictures

1539 Hernando de Soto

Motivations: I had one major reason for exploring Florida—to find gold. I had already found some in Mexico and thought that Florida would have it too. I also was supposed to start a colony and teach Christianity to Native Americans. But I didn't end up meeting any of my goals.

What I Did: My group explored much of the southwestern part of North America. We're famous for being the first Europeans to cross the Mississippi River. We failed at getting along with Native Americans, though, and our groups fought many times.

Interesting Fact: During my travels, I found a man who survived Pánfilo de Narváez's expedition, Juan Ortiz. Ortiz joined my group and helped us communicate with Native Americans.

Chart and Graph Skills

Use a Time Line

Remember that a time line shows the order in which events occurred. In each box, write the name of the explorer or explorers who came to Florida that year. Include at least two details about the explorers and their expeditions too.

| 1510 | 1520 | 1530 | 1540 |

1513

1528

1539

Who Am I?

Read the descriptions. Write the names of the explorers that are described on the lines.

1. I didn't have a choice whether to come to Florida or not. I was an enslaved man.

_____

2. I was the first Spanish conquistador in Florida. I tried to start a colony.

_____

3. I was searching for gold. I didn't find any, but I did cross the Mississippi River.

_____

4. My journal of my travels tells how I made it to Mexico.

_____

5. I was an African conquistador who wanted to find gold.

_____

6. My attempt at starting a colony and finding gold failed when I split up my force.

_____

Lesson 1

 Essential Question Why do people explore?

_____

_____

_____

_____

_____

_____

Go back to *Show As You Go!* on pages 40–41. «

Important Communities

(?) Essential Question

Why do people live where they live?

What do you think?

_____

_____

_____

_____

Words To Know

What do you think these words mean? Write your predictions on the lines.

***permanent**

_____

moat

_____

***opinion**

_____

militia

_____

NGSS Standards
SS.4.A.3.3 Identify the significance of St. Augustine as the oldest permanent European settlement in the United States.

Think about the community that you live in. How old do you think it is? Florida has some of the oldest communities in our country. In fact, one community in Florida is the oldest European one in the entire United States. You'll learn about how it started in this lesson.

Look at the three images of early communities in Florida below.

▼ Fort Caroline

▲ Fort Mose

▲ St. Augustine

1. Which of these three places do you think was the first permanent, or lasting, community?

St. Augustine

2. As you read this lesson, check to see if your answer was correct. If not, write the correct answer here:

_____

F. Delfinum

SuperStock

▲ **The French arriving in Florida**

The French in Florida

Until 1561, only one European country—Spain—had explored and tried to colonize Florida. As you have read, these first Spanish attempts at setting up communities didn't work. Soon, Spain faced another kind of challenge. France, another European country, landed in Florida and started to claim the area for itself.

The French came to Florida for many of the same reasons as the Spanish. They both were interested in any riches that Florida might have. The French also wanted to create colonies and control land. Religious reasons brought some French to Florida too. Unlike the Spanish, the French were not interested in teaching their religion to Native Americans. Instead, they came to Florida so that they could practice their own religion freely.

> **DID YOU KNOW?**
> The French who came to Florida for religious freedom were called Huguenots.

> **NGSS Standards**
> **SS.4.A.3.1** Identify explorers who came to Florida and the motivations for their expeditions.
> **SS.4.A.3.7** Identify nations (Spain, France, England) that controlled Florida before it became a United States territory.

Underline the reasons the French came to Florida.

57

NGSS Standards
SS.4.A.3.1 Identify explorers who came to Florida and the motivations for their expeditions.
SS.4.A.3.7 Identify nations (Spain, France, England) that controlled Florida before it became a United States territory.

First Colonies

As you will read below, from 1562 to 1565 Spain and France both tried to control Florida. France did create a settlement in Florida. However, it only lasted for a little over a year. Once the French settlement ended, Spain regained control of Florida. It would keep this control for the next 198 years.

Look at the blank squares next to each date.
• Put an X in the square if the events relate to France.
• Put a check in the square if the events relate to Spain.
• Put a star in the square if the events relate to both France and Spain.

1562 X

Jean Ribault landed in northern Florida. He claimed the area for France. His expedition continued north to the area that would become South Carolina. He created a settlement called Charlesfort there. It did not last, though. The settlement ran out of supplies, and the French sailed back home.

◀ This monument recognizes Ribault's landing near Jacksonville, Florida.

1564 X

René Goulaine de Laudonnière started the first French settlement in Florida. He named this settlement Fort Caroline. It was located on the St. Johns River. A **moat**, or a ditch filled with water that surrounds a fort, helped protect the settlement. The Timucua Native Americans helped the French.

▲ Fort Caroline

Put a box around the names of the **French** explorers who came to Florida.

1565 X

Life at Fort Caroline was hard. Supplies were low and people were hungry. Conflicts had developed between the French and the Timucua too. Many people wanted to give up and return to France. In August, help arrived. Jean Ribault returned to Florida from France with supplies and more people for the community.

1565

The Spanish king was upset that the French were in Florida. In his **opinion,** Florida belonged to Spain. So he sent Pedro Menéndez de Avilés to Florida. Menéndez's job was to get rid of the French and their community.

On August 28, Menéndez landed on the east coast of Florida. He created a community there called St. Augustine. It was the first permanent European community in what would become the United States. The stone fort that was built later in St. Augustine helped the community survive during its long history.

▲ The Spanish attacking Fort Caroline

1565

Ribault and the rest of the French saw Menéndez and the Spanish arrive in Florida. They knew that it was a matter of time before the Spanish attacked them. So the French decided to attack first. Ribault and his crew sailed toward St. Augustine, but disaster struck along the way—a hurricane destroyed their ships and left them stranded south of St. Augustine.

Pedro Menéndez de Avilés ▼

1565

Realizing that the French had left Fort Caroline weakly defended, Menéndez decided to attack it. He and his men killed most of the French there. Menéndez renamed the fort San Mateo and left a few soldiers there to guard it.

Menéndez returned to St. Augustine. Soon, he found the stranded Frenchmen and had them killed too.

NGSS Standards
SS.4.A.3.1 Identify explorers who came to Florida and the motivations for their expeditions. **SS.4.A.3.3** Identify the significance of St. Augustine as the oldest permanent European settlement in the United States. **SS.4.A.3.7** Identify nations (Spain, France, England) that controlled Florida before it became a United States territory.

Reading Skill

Understand Cause and Effect

Write two causes and their effects from the information on these pages.

Cause	Effect

National Geographic/Getty Images

DID YOU KNOW?
1. Fort Mose had its own **militia**. A militia is a military unit. It helped defend St. Augustine.
2. Francisco Menéndez, an African who had escaped enslavement, led the militia and was a leader of the community.

THINK · PAIR · SHARE
Find the word *loyalty* on this page. Tell a partner what you think this word means.

A Free African Community

About 175 years after St. Augustine was founded, another important community started in Florida. This community—Fort Mose—was the first settlement for free Africans in what would become the United States.

Africans had been in North America since the expedition of Juan Ponce de León. Many of these Africans were enslaved, and some of them decided to escape. In the late 1600s and early 1700s, the Spanish in Florida welcomed these runaways. The Spanish gave these Africans their freedom if they gave their loyalty to Spain and became Christians.

In 1738 the Spanish governor of Florida created Fort Mose for these Africans. The fort was located along a creek about two miles north of St. Augustine. The fort provided protection for St. Augustine because it could warn St. Augustine if an attack was coming.

NGSS Standards
SS.4.A.3.5 Identify the significance of Fort Mose as the first free African community in the United States.

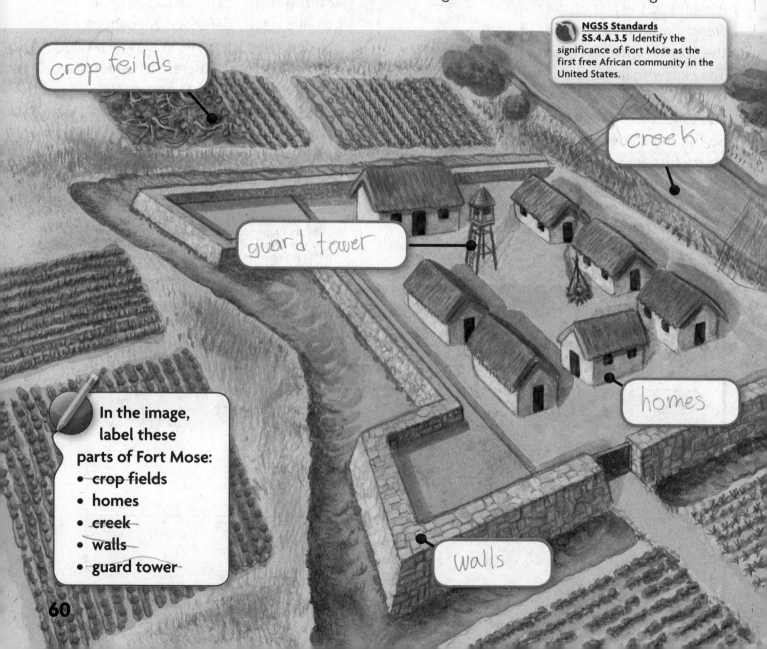

crop feilds

creek

guard tower

homes

walls

In the image, label these parts of Fort Mose:
• crop fields
• homes
• creek
• walls
• guard tower

60

▲ St. Augustine

Match It Up!

Draw lines to match these communities with their descriptions. Each number will match to more than one answer. One has been done for you.

1. Fort Caroline •

2. St. Augustine •

3. Fort Mose •

- French community in Florida started by Rene Laudonnière that lasted for only a short time

- first free African community in the United States

- Spanish community started by Pedro Menéndez

- community that included people who came to Florida for religious freedom

- community that received help from the Timucua

- community started in 1738 that had its own militia

- first permanent European community in the United States

- community located north of St. Augustine that took in formerly enslaved Africans

---

Lesson 2

 Essential Question Why do people live where they live?

_____

_____

_____

_____

Go back to *Show As You Go!* on pages 40–41. «««

 netw⊕rks connected.mcgraw-hill.com
○ Games ○ Assessment

Life on Spanish Missions

? Essential Question

What happens when cultures meet?

What do you think?

_____

_____

_____

_____

_____

_____

_____

_____

_____

_____

_____

Words To Know

Look at the words below. Tell a partner what you already know about these words.

mission
convert
*abandon

NGSS Standards
SS.4.A.3.4 Explain the purpose of and daily life on missions (San Luis de Talimali in present-day Tallahassee).

Do you like being the first one to do something? As you've read, our state of Florida has many of our country's firsts. Complete these firsts by filling in the lines below.

- *first place in the United States that Europeans*

_____

- *first _____ European community in the United States*

- *first free _____ community in the United States*

Here's another first for Florida—place with the first **mission**. A mission was a settlement where religion was taught. This first mission was called Nombre de Dios. It was created in 1565 near St. Augustine. It still stands today!

▼ **Nombre de Dios**

Missions

Native Americans had their own religions before the Spanish arrived. The Spanish set up missions to **convert** Native Americans to Christianity. To convert is to change your beliefs. After converting, Native Americans no longer followed many of their traditional beliefs. Instead, they mostly followed the teachings of Christianity.

At missions, the Spanish also wanted to teach Native Americans about the Spanish way of life. Native Americans learned to speak Spanish and to use Spanish tools. Native Americans started to dress like the Spanish as well. They learned how to grow and eat new foods that the Spanish brought to the Americas too.

▲ The leader of a mission was a person called a friar.

©Corbis

What was the purpose of missions?

To spread christianity and their culture.

NGSS Standards
SS.4.A.1.1 Analyze primary and secondary sources to identify significant individuals and events throughout Florida history.
SS.4.A.3.4 Explain the purpose of and daily life on missions (San Luis de Talimali in present-day Tallahassee).

Primary Source

Quote

". . . our principal intent [goal] in the discovery of new lands is that the inhabitants [people] . . . may be brought to understand the truth of our holy [Christian] Faith."

—Spanish King Charles V, 1532

Write what this quote means in your own words.

_____

_____

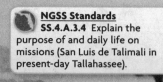
San Luis de Talimali

What was daily life like on a Spanish mission? We can find out by studying San Luis de Talimali mission. The Spanish and the Apalachee Native Americans lived there. It was located near present-day Tallahassee. This mission was one of the largest in Florida, and at its height in 1675, about 1,500 people lived there.

Spanish homes

blockhouse

fort

garden

animal pen

Work Life

A big part of daily life on the mission at San Luis involved growing crops and raising animals. People grew oranges, corn, wheat, watermelons, and many other crops. They raised pigs, cows, and chickens. The mission sent some of these items to St. Augustine and Spain every year.

Other kinds of work kept people busy too. The mission had weavers, leather makers, and metal workers. These workers made different kinds of useful items, such as clothing and metal tools. The mission also had soldiers who provided protection.

Homes and families also required a lot of work. People cooked, cleaned, did laundry, and cared for children.

In the image, circle the place where soldiers worked at San Luis.

Social Life

The people of San Luis also took time away from work. The Apalachee and the Spanish attended church services together every week. They also gathered at the mission's central plaza to trade and hold community meetings. The Apalachee sometimes used the plaza to play a ball game called pelota. The Apalachee used a building called the council house for their own gatherings and meetings too.

In the image, put a star on the place where someone could trade.

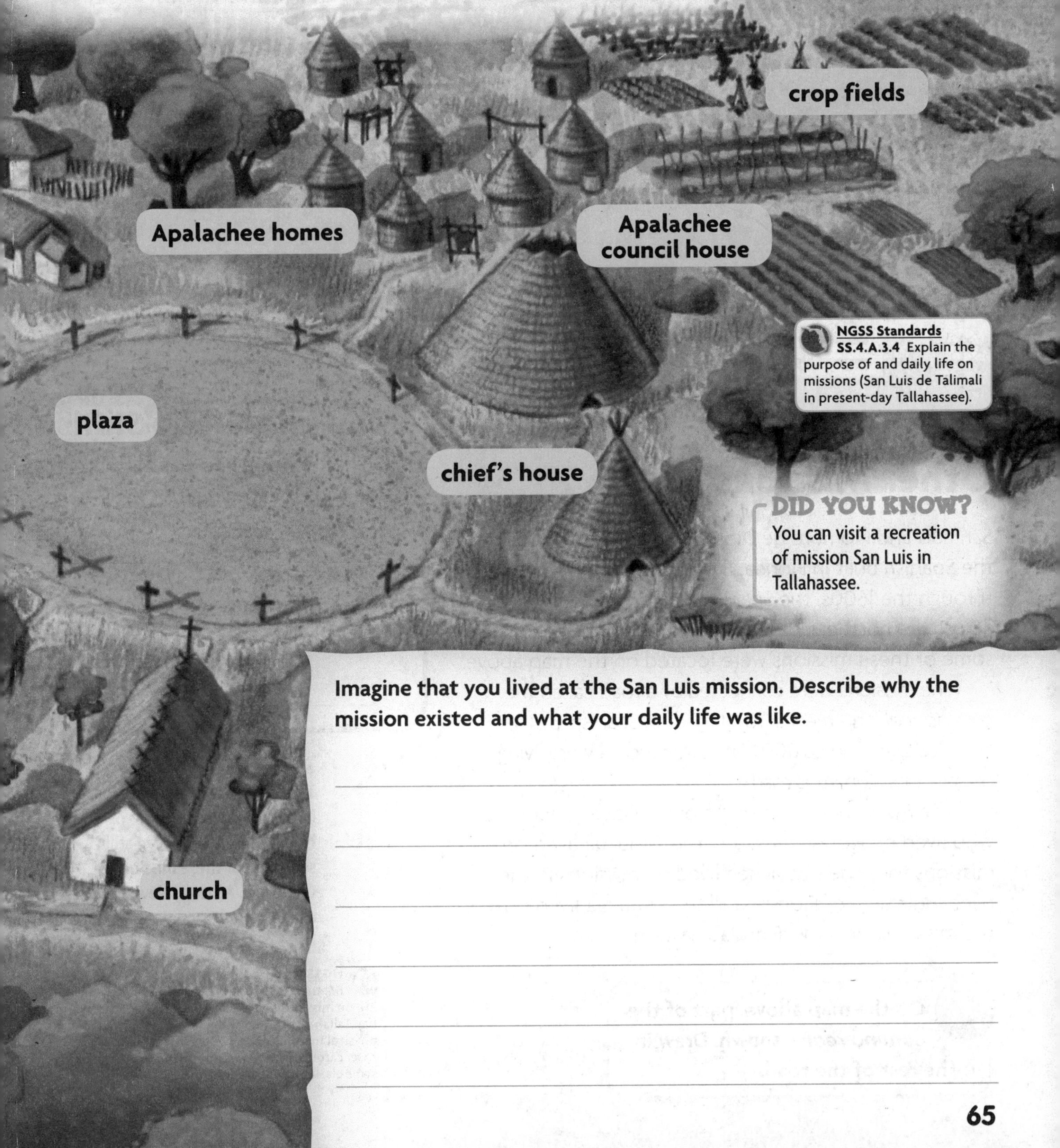

crop fields

Apalachee homes

Apalachee council house

NGSS Standards
SS.4.A.3.4 Explain the purpose of and daily life on missions (San Luis de Talimali in present-day Tallahassee).

plaza

chief's house

DID YOU KNOW?
You can visit a recreation of mission San Luis in Tallahassee.

church

Imagine that you lived at the San Luis mission. Describe why the mission existed and what your daily life was like.

_____

_____

_____

_____

_____

_____

GEORGIA

ALABAMA

81°W

ATLANTIC OCEAN

31°N

San Luis

Apalachicola River

30°N

Gulf of Mexico

Suwannee River

St. Johns River

Nombre de Dios

FLORIDA

N
W   E
S

Mission

Camino Real

0   20   40 miles

0   20   40 kilometers

85°W   84°W   83°W

29°N

Other Missions

San Luis and Nombre de Dios weren't the only missions the Spanish built in Florida. From the middle of the 1500s through the 1600s, the Spanish created many missions across the northern part of Florida. You can see where some of these missions were located on the map above.

The missions were connected by a road called the *camino real*. This means "royal road" in Spanish. By the late 1600s, around 20,000 Native Americans were living on missions along this road.

The Apalachee weren't the only Native Americans who lived on Florida missions. The Timucua lived on missions too. The Apalachee lived on missions in the panhandle area of Florida, and the Timucua lived on the missions closer to Florida's eastern coast.

On the map above, part of the *camino real* is shown. Draw in the rest of the road.

Map and Globe Skills

1. What latitude line was Nombre de Dios located near?

_____

2. About how far was San Luis from Nombre de Dios?

_____

DID YOU KNOW?

The Spanish also built missions in the southwestern part of North America. You can still see some of these missions in California, Arizona, New Mexico, and Texas.

NGSS Standards
SS.4.A.3.4 Explain the purpose of and daily life on missions (San Luis de Talimali in present-day Tallahassee). **SS.4.G.1.4** Interpret political and physical maps using map elements (title, compass rose, cardinal directions, intermediate directions, symbols, legend, scale, longitude, latitude).

Although many Native Americans converted to Christianity and learned Spanish ways, they kept parts of their own cultures too. For instance, the leaders of the Apalachee and Timucua still controlled everyday matters. After converting, the Apalachee and Timucua continued to follow some of their old religious beliefs in addition to their new Christian ones.

The missions had problems. The Spanish often made Native Americans work for them. Native Americans had to grow crops and raise animals for the Spanish. The Spanish also forced Native Americans to work on building projects. Over time, Spanish demands for labor became a form of slavery for Native Americans. Some Native Americans, though, fought back against the Spanish.

Disease was a problem on missions too. Thousands of Native Americans died from illnesses that they got from the Spanish. Some missions were also attacked by other Native Americans and other Europeans. As a result of these problems, by the early 1700s, most missions had been **abandoned.**

▲ One tradition that the Apalachee kept after converting to Christianity was playing pelota.

NGSS Standards
SS.4.A.3.2 Describe causes and effects of European colonization on the Native American tribes of Florida.

What effects did the missions have on Native Americans?

_____

Lesson **3**

 Essential Question What happens when cultures meet?

_____

_____

_____

Go back to _Show As You Go!_ on pages 40–41. «

 **netwⓍrks**

There's More Online!
◉ Games ◉ Assessment

Europe Fights Over Florida

(?) Essential Question

Why does control of an area change?

What do you think?

_____

_____

_____

_____

_____

_____

_____

Words To Know

Look at the words below. Circle the words you already know. Put question marks next to the words you don't know.

_____ **treaty**

_____ ***support**

_____ ***general**

NGSS Standards
SS.4.A.3.7 Identify nations (Spain, France, England) that controlled Florida before it became a United States territory.

68

Have you ever had someone give you one of their games as a gift to keep? If so, you know that the game used to belong to them, but now you own it. Control of the game changed.

Control of Florida has changed several times during its history. Three different European countries have controlled the area at one time or another.

Look at the three flags. Which country controlled Florida first? Put a #1 next to its flag.

France

Spain

England

DID YOU KNOW?
Spain controlled Florida for close to 300 years. In fact, Florida was controlled by Spain for longer than it has been part of the United States.

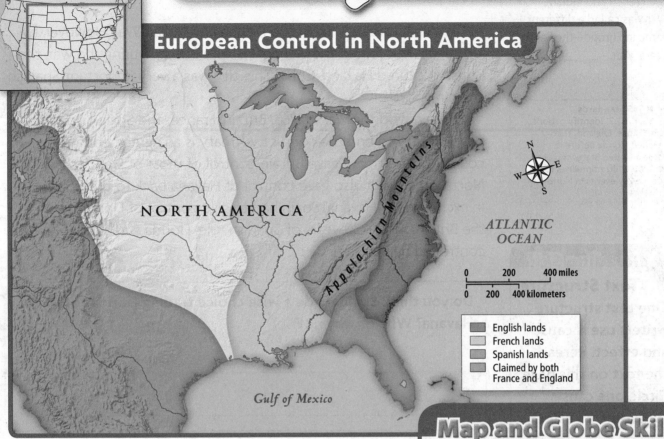

European Control in North America

NORTH AMERICA

Appalachian Mountains

ATLANTIC OCEAN

Gulf of Mexico

| | 0   200   400 miles |
| | 0   200   400 kilometers |

■ English lands
□ French lands
■ Spanish lands
■ Claimed by both France and England

European Countries in Florida

As you have read, Spain's control of Florida started in 1513. Then, France was in Florida between 1562 and 1565. After the Spanish destroyed Fort Caroline, Spain regained control.

Another European country, England, also had an interest in North America. While Spain had been building colonies in Florida, England had been busy creating its own colonies. These English colonies were located north of Florida.

In 1756 England, which was also called Great Britain, went to war with the French and Native Americans over control of land west of the Appalachian Mountains. This war was called the French and Indian War. It brought a change to which country controlled Florida.

1. Put a box around the dates that France was in Florida.

2. Why did the French and Indian War start?

_____

_____

Map and Globe Skills

True or False? France controlled land east of the Appalachian Mountains.

_____

NGSS Standards
SS.4.A.3.7 Identify nations (Spain, France, England) that controlled Florida before it became a United States territory.
SS.4.G.1.4 Interpret political and physical maps using map elements (title, compass rose, cardinal directions, intermediate directions, symbols, legend, scale, longitude, latitude).

NGSS Standards
SS.4.A.3.7 Identify nations (Spain, France, England) that controlled Florida before it became a United States territory.
SS.4.A.9.1 Utilize timelines to sequence key events in Florida history.

Florida Changes Hands

At first, Spain stayed out of the French and Indian War. However, by 1762 Spain had joined the war against the British. During the war, the British captured Havana, Cuba. This city was a very important Spanish shipping port.

Britain won the war in 1763. Britain, France, and Spain signed a peace **treaty** to end the conflict. A treaty is an agreement among countries. The treaty gave Britain control of most of France's land in North America. It also gave control of Havana back to the Spanish. In exchange for Havana, Spain had to give control of Florida to the British. After 250 years of Spanish rule, Florida was suddenly controlled by England.

Reading Skill
Text Structure
One text structure writers use is cause and effect. Reread the text on this page. Circle one cause. Underline its effect.

> **Do you think Spain made a wise choice trading Florida for Havana? Why or why not?**
>
> _____
>
> _____

Chart and Graph Skills

Use a Time Line
Look at the legend to the right. Use these colors to color in the time line below to show when each country controlled Florida. Then answer the question.

■ Spain
■ France
■ England

How long did England control Florida?

_____

| 1513 | 1562 | 1565 | 1763 | 1783 |

1513
Juan Ponce de León lands in Florida.

1562
Jean Ribault lands in Florida.

1565
St. Augustine is founded.

1763
The French and Indian War ends.

1783
The American Revolution ends.

Florida didn't stay under British control for very long. In 1776 the British colonies to the north of Florida declared their independence from Britain. The American Revolution had begun.

In 1779 the Spanish joined the war on the side of the Americans. To **support** the Americans, Spanish **general** Bernardo de Gálvez attacked places that Britain controlled, including Pensacola, Florida. This city fell to the Spanish after a two-month battle.

The Americans won the war in 1783. As part of the treaty for this war, Britain gave Florida back to the Spanish. Florida was under Spanish rule once again.

▲ George Washington (center) led the American soldiers during the American Revolution.

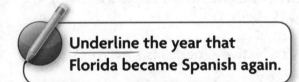

Underline the year that Florida became Spanish again.

NGSS Standards
SS.4.A.3.7 Identify nations (Spain, France, England) that controlled Florida before it became a United States territory.

Lesson 4

❓ **Essential Question** Why does control of an area change?

_____

_____

_____

_____

_____

_____

Go back to *Show As You Go!* on pages 40–41.

connected.mcgraw-hill.com
● Games ● Assessment

Library of Congress

Effects of European Rule

(?) Essential Question

What happens when cultures meet?
What do you think?

_____

_____

_____

_____

Words To Know

What do you think these words mean? Write your answers on the lines.

agriculture

_____

_____

_____

*expose

_____

_____

_____

_____

NGSS Standards
SS.4.A.3.2 Describe causes and effects of European colonization on the Native American tribes of Florida.

72

Has a new family ever moved into your neighborhood? Maybe you became friends with the kids in this family. Or you learned how to make a special food from these new neighbors. Your life changed because new people arrived.

The lives of Native Americans changed a lot when new people—the Europeans—arrived. In fact, the lives of Native Americans would never be the same again once Europeans set foot in Florida.

THINK · PAIR · SHARE

During this unit, you've learned about the causes of European colonization of Florida. With a partner, think about each phrase below. Circle yes if the phrase is a cause of European colonization. Circle no if the phrase is not a cause of colonization.

1. spread Christianity to Native Americans   (yes)   no

2. find gold, silver, and other riches   (yes)   no

3. teach Native Americans about European culture   yes   (no)

4. learn how to speak Native American languages   yes   (no)

5. create colonies   (yes)   no

6. create the United States of America   yes   (no)

Share and discuss your answers with your entire class.

▲ Cattle have been in Florida for over 400 years.

Effects of Spanish Rule

You've read that Spain controlled Florida for a long time—almost 300 years, in fact. This rule left a lasting effect on our state.

Agriculture

One of the largest effects of Spanish rule in Florida has to do with **agriculture**. Agriculture is the farming of crops and the raising of animals. The Spanish brought new kinds of crops and animals to Florida. Did you know that the Spanish brought the first oranges and cattle to Florida? The Spanish also introduced watermelons, peaches, peas, wheat, and garbanzo beans (also called chick peas) to Florida. They brought pigs, chickens, sheep, goats, and horses too.

Spanish Names

Some of the names of places in our state are an effect of Spanish rule. Many Florida cities got their current names from their original Spanish ones. These cities include St. Augustine, St. Marks, and St. Joseph. Many streets in Florida have Spanish names as well.

▲ Punta Gorda is a city in Florida with a Spanish name.

Weapons

Spanish rule changed the kinds of weapons people in Florida used. Before the Spanish arrived in Florida, Native Americans used wooden tools and weapons. The Spanish brought their metal weapons with them to Florida. The Native Americans wanted these weapons because metal is stronger than wood. So Native Americans traded with the Spanish for weapons. These items included knives, guns, and cannons.

▲ Spanish gun

Underline the kinds of agriculture that the Spanish brought to Florida.

NGSS Standards
SS.4.A.3.6 Identify the effects of Spanish rule in Florida.

73

(t) CORBIS, (cr) © Ilene MacDonald / Alamy

Missions were built on Native American land ▶

▲ European glass beads

Effects on Native Americans

As you've read, the arrival of Europeans in Florida greatly changed the lives of Native Americans. A few changes were good and made life easier. However, most changes caused problems for the Native Americans.

Culture

Native Americans' way of life changed—for good and for bad—because of Spanish colonization. For example, Native Americans gained new goods and ways of doing things. Through trade, Native Americans got metal tools and weapons, glass beads, and other European items. As you've read, Native Americans also learned about Spanish agriculture and used Spanish language and clothing. These new items and methods usually made life easier for Native Americans.

However, by taking on parts of Spanish culture, Native Americans lost many of their traditional ways of living. For example, as you have read, many Native Americans converted to Christianity. When they converted, many Native Americans stopped following many of the traditional beliefs that they had held for thousands of years.

 Fill in the boxes below with the causes and effects of European colonization and rule of Florida.

Causes of Colonization	Effects of Colonization

Conflict

Fighting and violence between Native Americans and Europeans was another bad effect of colonization. Native Americans fought to defend themselves and their land. Europeans fought back to gain control of this same land. Many people, both Native Americans and Europeans, died during these conflicts. Native Americans usually lost these fights, and as a result, they lost much of their land too. Many had to move to new areas to live.

▲ **Native Americans and Europeans often fought.**

Disease

Disease had a huge—and negative—impact on Native Americans. When Europeans arrived in Florida, they carried many deadly germs with them. Native Americans had never been **exposed** to these germs before. As a result, Native Americans easily caught these illnesses. Thousands and thousands of Native Americans died from diseases like measles and smallpox. After Europeans arrived, the Native American population greatly decreased over time.

NGSS Standards
SS.4.A.3.2 Describe causes and effects of European colonization on the Native American tribes of Florida.

Slavery

Slavery was another negative effect of colonization. Some Europeans captured Native Americans and forced them into slavery. The Spanish, as you've read, required Native Americans to work for them on missions. Over time this work became a form of slavery.

Native Americans working at a mission. ▶

Lesson 5

(?) Essential Question   What happens when cultures meet?

_____

_____

_____

Go back to *Show As You Go!* on pages 40–41. ◀◀◀

networks **There's More Online!**
● Games ● Assessment

Complete the crossword puzzle below.

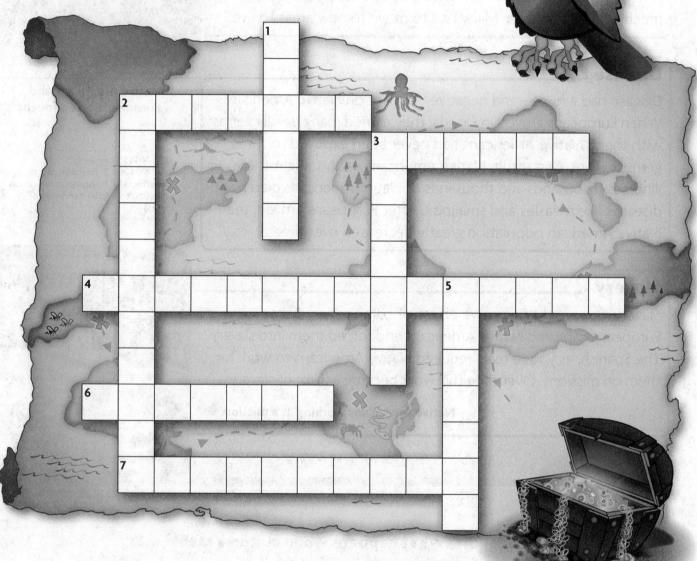

ACROSS

2 the practice of treating people as property and forcing them to work

3 place that is ruled by another country

4 first conquistador in Florida

6 settlement where religion was taught

7 journey for a special purpose

DOWN

1 an agreement among countries

2 first permanent European settlement in North America

3 to change your beliefs

5 country that controlled Florida at one time

April 1513

We've been sailing for almost a month now. Juan Ponce de León thinks that we should make landfall very soon. I'm glad because I'm ready to get off this ship and be on solid ground again. I'm also ready to start my search for gold.

Unit Project

Choose one of the European explorers that you have read about in this unit. Imagine that you are a member of his expedition to Florida. Create a travel log, or journal, about your journey. Before you begin writing, look back at **Show As You Go!** on pages 40–41 to review your notes. Also read the list below to see what information should be included in your travel log. As you work, check off each item as you include it.

Your travel log should include...   **Yes, it does!**

at least five entries.

the dates of your journey.

information about why you came to Florida.

information about the communities you visited.

information on the effects of your journey on Native Americans.

information on the challenges you faced.

at least two illustrations of your journey.

Think about the Big Idea

BIG IDEA People's actions affect others.

What did you learn in this unit that helps you understand the Big Idea?

_____

_____

_____

_____

Read the passage "Estéban Dorantes Helps Out" and then answer Numbers 1 through 3.

Estéban Dorantes Helps Out

1 PÁNFILO de Narváez brought a crew of Spanish explorers to Florida in 1528. They came to search for gold, but their expedition was a disaster. The men decided to leave. They built rafts and set sail west from Florida. As they got close to Texas, a storm wrecked their flimsy rafts. De Narváez and many others drowned!

2 Enslaved African Estéban Dorantes was one of the survivors. Dorantes helped the remaining crew find a way to the Spanish colony of Mexico. Throughout their trip across Texas and into Mexico, Dorantes made friends with the Native Americans. These peaceful relationships helped the crew travel safely through Native American communities.

3 The group finally reached Mexico City eight years after they began their trip. There they told their tale of adventure. The governor of Mexico, who was from Spain, was very interested in the stories about Native Americans in the north. He thought these Native Americans might have riches or know where to find them. The stories of the survivors encouraged other Spanish explorers to continue to search for gold in the Americas. The governor of Mexico sent Dorantes on one of these expeditions in 1539. Dorantes didn't make it back from this expedition to northern Mexico, however. He was killed by Native Americans.

"Estéban Dorantes Helps Out" property of McGraw-Hill Education.

GO ON →

Now answer questions 1 through 3. Base your answers on the passage "Estéban Dorantes Helps Out."

1 Fill in the circle **before** the sentence from the passage which best explains the importance of Dorantes' relationship with the Native Americans.

Ⓐ Enslaved African Estéban Dorantes was one of the survivors. Ⓑ Dorantes helped the remaining crew find a way to the Spanish colony of Mexico. Ⓒ Throughout their trip across Texas and into Mexico, Dorantes made friends with the Native Americans. Ⓓ These peaceful relationships helped the crew travel safely through Native American communities.

2 Read this sentence from paragraph 1.

"As they got close to Texas, a storm wrecked their flimsy rafts."

What does the word <u>flimsy</u> mean as it is used in this sentence?

Ⓐ clean

Ⓑ dirty

Ⓒ strong

Ⓓ weak

3 Why did Spanish explorers continue to search for gold in North America?

Ⓐ They were ordered to do so by the king.

Ⓑ They wanted to find Pánfilo de Narváez.

Ⓒ They were encouraged by the stories the survivors told.

Ⓓ They needed to defend Mexico against Native Americans.

GO ONLINE to connected.mcgraw-hill.com for enhanced Florida Test Preparation options, available through Engrade.

BIG IDEA Conflict causes change.

In the early 1800s, conflicts in Florida brought about many changes. One conflict gave control of Florida to the United States. Other conflicts forced Native Americans to move out of Florida. The biggest conflict in American history, the Civil War, changed the way of life of African Americans and many others throughout the South. As you read this unit, think about the changes that happened because of these conflicts. Does war always lead to change?

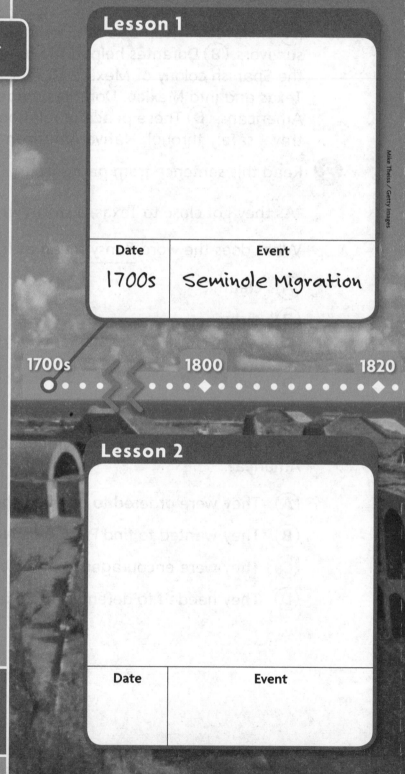

Lesson 1

Date	Event
1700s	Seminole Migration

1700s ••••• 1800 •••••••••••• 1820

Lesson 2

Date	Event

Mike Theiss / Getty Images

networks

connected.mcgraw-hill.com
- Skill Builders
- Vocabulary Flashcards

Show As You Go! After you read each lesson, choose an important event from that lesson. Draw a picture to represent the event in the related lesson box. Be sure to include the year and name of the event. Then, draw a line from the box to the correct year on the time line. Part of the first lesson has been done for you. By the end of the unit, you will have a time line of Florida's early history!

Fold page here.

Lesson 3

Date	Event

Lesson 5

Date	Event

1840   1860   1880   1900

Lesson 4

Date	Event

Lesson 6

Date	Event

Fort Jackson at Garden Key, Florida

Reading Skill

NGSS Standards
LAFS.4.RI.2.6 Compare and contrast a firsthand and secondhand account of the same event or topic; describe the differences in focus and the information provided.
SS.4.A.1.1 Analyze primary and secondary sources to identify significant individuals and events throughout Florida history.

Compare and Contrast Firsthand and Secondhand Accounts

Firsthand accounts are a type of primary source. A firsthand account is written or made by someone who witnessed an event. Secondhand accounts are another name for secondary sources. These accounts are made or written by people who analyze primary sources.

In Unit 3, you'll be learning about Florida's early history. Comparing and contrasting firsthand and secondhand accounts from this time period will help you understand our state's history.

◀ Andrew Jackson

Similarities
The U.S. government provided wagons to move Native Americans west.

Differences
The primary source views Indian removal as sadness for Native Americans. The secondary source notes that the reason for Indian removal was to end conflicts.

LEARN IT

- To compare two or more things, note how they are similar, or alike.

- To contrast two or more things, note how they are different.

- Read the passages below. Think about how they may be about the same event or topic but still may have differences in focus and description.

Read the two accounts below about the removal of Native Americans who lived east of the Mississippi River in 1838.

Firsthand account: An eyewitness to Indian removal in 1838

I saw [Native Americans] loaded like cattle or sheep into six hundred and forty-five wagons and started toward the west. . . . the children rose to their feet and waved their little hands good-by to their mountain homes, knowing they were leaving forever.

Secondhand account: Encyclopedia

President Andrew Jackson was in favor of removing Native Americans who lived east of the Mississippi River to the Indian Territory. The U.S. government provided wagons to move Native Americans to the Indian Territory, but many had to walk. Jackson believed it would put an end to conflicts between Native Americans and settlers in the area.

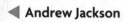

Library of Congress

TRY IT

You can use a Venn diagram to help you compare and contrast accounts. Fill in the chart with the similarities and differences from the accounts on page 82. Write the similarities of the accounts in the center of the diagram.

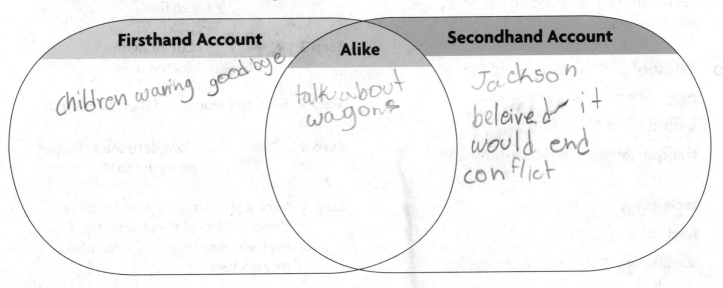

Firsthand Account

children waving good bye

Alike

talk about wagons

Secondhand Account

Jackson beleived it would end conflict

APPLY IT

- Review the steps for comparing and contrasting in Learn It.
- Read the accounts below about the battle of Olustee during the Civil War.

Then circle the similarities and underline the differences in the accounts.

The Confederate Victory at Olustee

Primary Source: Report from Brigadier-General Joseph Finegan

"The enemy retreated that night hastily and in some confusion, to Sanderson, leaving a large number of their killed and wounded in our possession on the field. . . . The victory was complete and the enemy retired in rapid retreat, [leaving] in quick succession . . . and falling back on Jacksonville."

Secondary Source: a book on the battle of Olustee

For six hours on February 20 these two armies were locked in battle among the pines near Olustee. The victory was complete and the enemy retreated rapidly to Jacksonville. The railroad bridge was saved from destruction.

Words to Know

NGSS Standards
LAFS.4.RI.2.4 Determine the meaning of general academic and domain-specific words or phrases in a text relevant to a grade 4 topic or subject area.

The list below shows some important words you will learn in this unit. Their definitions can be found on the next page. Read the words.

territory (TER·uh·tawr·ee) (p. 92)

reservation (reh·zuhr·VAY·shuhn) (p. 94)

cash crop (KASH KRAHP) (p. 99)

transportation (trans·puhr·TAY·shuhn) (p. 103)

technology (tek·NAH·luh·jee) (p. 103)

ford (FORD) (p. 103)

abolitionist (a·buh·LIH·shuhn·ihst) (p. 107)

sharecropping (SHEHR·krah·ping) (p. 117)

FOLDABLES®

The **Foldable** on the next page will help you learn these important words. Follow the steps below to make your Foldable.

Step 1 Fold along the solid red line.

Step 2 Cut along the dotted lines.

Step 3 Read the words and their definitions.

Step 4 Complete the activities on each tab.

Step 5 Look at the back of your Foldable. Choose ONE of these activities for each word to help you remember its meaning:

- Draw a picture of the word.
- Write a description of the word.
- Write how the word is related to something you know.

(l) Royalty-Free/CORBIS

A **territory** is an area of land controlled by a nation.	Write the plural form of *territory*. territories
A **reservation** is an area of land set aside for Native Americans.	Write the root word of *reservation*. reserve
A **cash crop** is a crop grown to be sold for profit.	Write two examples of cash crops. sugar cane pumpkin
Transportation is the way in which people and goods are moved from place to place.	Circle the examples of transportation. (cars) (bicycle) houses farms (ships) (railroads)
Technology is the use of skills, ideas, and tools to meet people's needs.	What is your favorite type of technology? TV
A **ford** is a shallow place where a river or stream may be crossed.	Write two words that rhyme with *ford*. lord board
An **abolitionist** is a person who wanted to end slavery in the United States.	Write the root word of *abolitionist*. ablish
Sharecropping is a system in which farmers rented land in return for a portion of the crops they grew.	Write the word *sharecropping*. Circle the two smaller words found in the word. 

FOLD

territory	**territory**
	CUT HERE
reservation	**reservation**
cash crop	**cash crop**
transportation	**transportation**
technology	**technology**
ford	**ford**
abolitionist	**abolitionist**
sharecropping	**sharecropping**

Primary Sources

NGSS Standards
SS.4.A.1.1 Analyze primary and secondary sources to identify significant individuals and events throughout Florida history.

Paintings

Library of Congress Prints and Photographs Division Washington - D.C. 20540 USA

Artists often create paintings of historical events and people. Paintings can show what life was like in the past. Paintings can be either primary or secondary sources. Paintings made by witnesses of a place or event are primary sources. Paintings that are based on primary sources to recreate an event or place are secondary sources.

In this unit, you'll learn about the lives of pioneers in Florida in the early 1800s. Paintings of this time period can help you understand how pioneers lived.

 Document-Based Questions

The painting on this page is from the 1800s and shows a settler's blockhouse. Study the painting and answer the questions below.

1. **What information would you need to know to determine if this painting is a primary source?**

   _____

   _____

2. **Describe what is happening in the painting.**

   _____

   _____

3. **What does this painting tell you about pioneer life?**

   _____

   _____

networks
There's More Online!
● Skill Builders
● Resource Library

The Seminole

 Essential Question

What happens when cultures meet?
What do you think?

_____

_____

_____

_____

_____

_____

Words To Know

Pick the symbol that shows how much you know about the meaning of each word below. Draw the symbol next to the word.

? = I have no idea!
▲ = I know a little.
★ = I know a lot.

_____ **migrate**

_____ ***perform**

NGSS Standards
SS.4.A.3.8 Explain how the Seminole tribe formed and the purpose for their migration.
SS.4.G.1.4 Interpret political and physical maps using map elements (title, compass rose, cardinal directions, intermediate directions, symbols, legend, scale, longitude, latitude)

Have you ever had to move from one home to another? Do you think moving is difficult? Why or why not? Write your thoughts below.

I think moving is hard because of all the packing, leaving all your friends, and all the driving.

In the 1700s, a group of Native Americans called the Creek lived in Alabama and Georgia. They often fought with other Native American tribes and Europeans in the area. Several small groups of Creek decided they wanted to live in peace. They broke away from the Creek and migrated to northern Florida. To **migrate** is to move from one place to another. The Spanish in Florida welcomed the Creek, who had been enemies of the British. The Spanish hoped that the Creek would help protect Spanish Florida. The population of Spanish Florida was low. Spanish leaders hoped that the Creek would add to their numbers, making them strong.

(Circle) the reason the Creek decided to migrate to Florida.

▼ **Lake Bradford in Tallahassee**

Comstock/PunchStock

Once in Florida, these Creek joined other Native Americans who already lived in the area. These Native Americans included the Apalachee and Tequesta who you read about in Unit 2. By the mid-1700s, this combined group of Native Americans had become known as the Seminole. No one knows for sure, but this name may have come from a Spanish word that means "wild one" or "runaway." The Seminole believe that their name comes from a Creek word that means "free people."

The Seminole created settlements in northern Florida. They lived like other Native American tribes in northern Florida and **performed** the same jobs. Men hunted and fished. Women farmed and made clothing. They used canoes to fish and travel along waterways. Some Seminole raised cattle. Trading was very important to the Seminole. They exchanged animal skins and furs for European goods, including knives, tools, and cloth.

FUN FACT
Every Seminole belonged to a clan, or family group. Most clans had animal names, such as alligator or bear. Children belonged to their mother's clan.

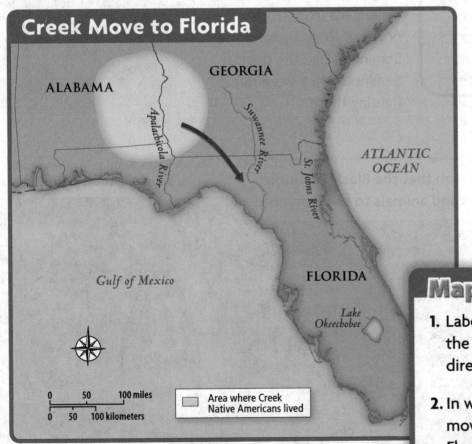

Creek Move to Florida

ALABAMA

GEORGIA

Apalachicola River

Suwannee River

St. Johns River

ATLANTIC OCEAN

Gulf of Mexico

FLORIDA

Lake Okeechobee

0   50   100 miles
0   50   100 kilometers

Area where Creek Native Americans lived

Map and Globe Skills

1. Label the compass rose with the cardinal and intermediate directions.

2. In what direction did the Creek move when they migrated to Florida?

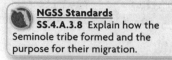

The Black Seminole

In the 1700s, the Seminole worked and lived closely with a group called the Black Seminole. The Black Seminole were Africans who had escaped from slavery. Remember that Europeans had been enslaving Africans in North America since the 1500s. In particular, the British used enslaved workers on plantations in their Southern colonies. Wanting their freedom, some enslaved workers chose to escape. Some migrated to Florida and lived alongside the Seminole.

The Seminole protected the Black Seminole from people who wanted to enslave them. In return, the Black Seminole gave part of the crops and animals they raised each year to the Seminole.

Over time, more Native Americans from lands north of Florida joined the Seminole. Like the original Seminole, they were fleeing fighting there.

Reading Skill

Understand Cause and Effect

1. What caused the Black Seminole to form a tribe?

_____

_____

_____

2. What effect did fighting in lands north of Florida have on Florida?

_____

_____

🖊 Put a box around the reason that the Black Seminole gave some of their crops and animals to the Seminole.

A Black Seminole (above) and a Seminole town (below)

The Seminole in Florida

 Draw a line to match each question with the correct answer.

Why did the Spanish welcome the Creek to Florida?

for travel and fishing

What Native American groups did the Creek join to form the Seminole?

animal skins and furs

How did the Seminole use rivers?

They wanted more people in Florida.

What did the Seminole trade for European goods?

crops and animals

Apalachee and Tequesta

What did the Black Seminole give to the Seminole in return for protection?

Lesson 1

 Essential Question What happens when cultures meet?

_____

_____

_____

_____

_____

_____

Go back to *Show As You Go!* on pages 80–81. «««

 netw✺rks
There's More Online!
● Games ● Assessment

Essential Question

How does control of an area change?

What do you think?

_____

_____

_____

_____

Library of Congress, Prints and Photographs Division [LC-USZC2-2753]

Words To Know

Write a number on each line to show how much you know about the meaning of each word below.

1 = I have no idea!
2 = I know a little.
3 = I know a lot.

____ **territory**

____ **planter**

____ ***organize**

____ **reservation**

____ ***propose**

NGSS Standards
SS.4.A.3.9 Explain how Florida (Adams-Onis Treaty) became a U.S. territory. **SS.4.A.3.10** Identify the causes and effects of the Seminole Wars.

In Unit 2 you read how a treaty is an agreement between nations. Have you ever made an agreement? What was the result of your agreement? Write your thoughts below.

_____

_____

_____

_____

In this lesson, you will learn about how the United States and Spain entered into a treaty which made Florida a U.S. **territory**. A territory is an area of land controlled by a nation. Read on to find out why Spain and the United States agreed to this treaty.

John Quincy Adams signed a treaty that made Florida a U.S. territory. ▼

NGSS Standards
SS.4.A.3.9 Explain how Florida (Adams-Onís Treaty) became a U.S. territory. **SS.4.A.3.10** Identify the causes and effects of the Seminole Wars.

The Adams-Onís Treaty

In the early 1800s, the Spanish government was having problems with Florida. Spain was busy fighting expensive wars in other parts of the world, and there were few soldiers available to control Florida. As a result, Spanish Florida had little law and order.

At the same time, Spain knew that many Americans wanted the United States to take control of Florida. There were a couple of reasons for this. First, many U.S. settlers in Georgia and other nearby areas wanted to settle on fertile land in northern Florida where the Seminole lived. Also, some American **planters**, or plantation owners, were upset that the Seminole protected escaped enslaved workers. As a result, the United States Army invaded Spanish Florida to fight the Seminole several times. These battles took place between 1817 and 1818 and came to be known as the First Seminole War.

During the First Seminole War, General Andrew Jackson entered Florida with an army of 3,000 men. Within a few months, many of the Seminole living along Georgia's border with Florida were killed. The survivors fled south. During this war, Spain saw the strength of the American army. The Spanish government did not think it could defeat them. So, Spain agreed to sign a treaty. On February 22, 1819, Spain and the United States signed the Adams-Onís Treaty. This treaty made Florida a U.S. territory.

Circle the cause of the First Seminole War. Underline its effect.

Draw a box around why Spain signed the Adams-Onís Treaty.

General Andrew Jackson during the transfer of power from the Spanish in Florida on July 10, 1821 ▼

93

The Florida Territory

Even though the Adams-Onís Treaty was signed in 1819, several years passed before it became official. In 1821 General Andrew Jackson became the military governor of the Florida territory. It was Jackson's job to **organize** the transfer of power from Spain to the United States.

The Adams-Onís Treaty became final on March 30, 1822. William P. Duval served as the first governor of the territory. Leaders named the capital of the territory Tallahassee, a Seminole word that means "old field."

The Seminole Reservation

The Florida territory quickly grew as American settlers poured into the area. As new white settlers claimed land, many Seminole were forced to move from their homes. As a result, tensions between the Seminole and the new settlers increased even more. In response, Governor Duval set up a **reservation** for the Seminole in central Florida in 1823. A reservation is an area of land set aside for Native Americans. The Seminole were unhappy about moving to the reservation, but many felt they had no choice. By 1827, most had moved.

> **Underline** why Governor Duval set up a reservation for the Seminole.

Seminole Lands, 1750–1842

ATLANTIC OCEAN

Pensacola
Tallahassee
St. Augustine

Gulf of Mexico

Lake Okeechobee
Everglades

N W E S

0   50   100 miles
0   50   100 kilometers

- Seminole lands, 1750
- Seminole lands, 1827
- Seminole lands, 1842

Map and Globe Skills

1. In what part of Florida did most Seminoles live in 1750?

   _____

2. Label the Seminole Reservation on the map.

3. Where did the Seminole live in 1842?

   _____

NGSS Standards
SS.4.A.3.9 Explain how Florida (Adams-Onis Treaty) became a U.S. territory. **SS.4.G.1.2** Locate and label cultural features on a Florida map. **SS.4.G.1.4** Interpret political and physical maps using map elements (title, compass rose, cardinal directions, intermediate directions, symbols, legend, scale, longitude, latitude)

The Second Seminole War

By 1830, the situation had become even worse for the Seminole. That year the U.S. government **proposed** and later passed a law which created an Indian Territory in what is today Oklahoma. This law tried to force all Native Americans living east of the Mississippi River to give up their land and move to the new territory. Many people in the government believed this would allow settlers to move into the area east of the Mississippi and prevent further conflicts with Native Americans.

The Seminole didn't want to move to the Indian Territory. They wanted to keep their way of life in Florida. The Seminole formed an army. The United States sent thousands of troops to Florida and spent millions of dollars on the war. In 1837 the U.S. Army also sent 4,000 troops to destroy crops, hoping to starve the Seminole into surrender.

In the end, about 4,000 Seminole surrendered. They were sent to the Indian Territory. About 300 Seminole, though, refused to surrender or leave Florida. They continued to live in the Everglades.

DID YOU KNOW?
In 1836 the United States government had a budget of 25 million dollars. The Second Seminole War cost the government about 30 million dollars. That means the war alone cost more than it cost to run the entire government for one year!

Underline why the Seminole did not want to move to the Indian Territory.

The United States sent thousands of troops to Florida during the Seminole Wars. ▼

LMR Group/Alamy

NGSS Standards
SS.4.A.3.8 Explain how the Seminole tribe formed and the purpose for their migration.
SS.4.A.3.10 Identify the causes and effects of the Seminole Wars.

Third Seminole War

In the 1850s, Indian removal was still an issue in Florida. The U.S. government felt the only way to move the remaining Seminole to the Indian Territory was to force them into battle.

A group of white men entered a Seminole camp on December 18, 1855 to try to make the Seminole attack first. In response, Seminole chief Holata Micco, also known as Billy Bowlegs, led an attack on a U.S. military camp on December 20. This attack began the Third Seminole War. This war was much smaller than the Second Seminole War, with fewer deaths and less fighting.

After three years of war, the U.S. military brought a group of Seminole from the Indian Territory to talk with Billy Bowlegs. On May 7, 1858, in exchange for money and Seminole land in the Indian Territory, Bowlegs agreed to end the war. Not all of the Seminole moved to the Indian Territory, however. Some still remained in the Everglades.

DID YOU KNOW?
Today, the Seminole Tribe of Florida is headquartered in Hollywood, Florida. They call themselves the "unconquered" because they never surrendered to the United States government.

Reading Skill

Compare and Contrast

Underline how the Third Seminole War was different from the Second Seminole War.

Billy Bowlegs was one of the last Native American leaders to resist relocation to the Indian Territory. ▶

(r) Library of Congress, (l) Zee/Alamy

Events of the Seminole Wars

 Fill in the chart with the causes and effects of each Seminole war.

	Cause	Effect
First Seminole War		
Second Seminole War		
Third Seminole War		

Lesson 2

 Essential Question How does control of an area change?

_____

_____

_____

_____

Go back to *Show As You Go!* on pages 80–81.

 netw⊙rks **There's More Online!** ● Games ● Assessment

Pioneer Life

How do people adapt?
What do you think?

_____

_____

_____

_____

_____

_____

_____

_____

_____

Have you ever gone camping? If you have, you know that you do not have all of the comforts of home while camping. Instead of sleeping in a house, you sleep in a tent. Instead of using a stove, you might build a campfire and roast hot dogs or marshmallows.

What would you do to improve your way of life if you lived at a campsite all year long?

_____

_____

If there were no stores, how would you find food?

_____

_____

_____

In the early 1800s, life on small farms in Florida was a lot like camping in the wilderness. But instead of pitching a tent, early settlers built log cabins to live in all year round. Instead of driving to a camp site, early settlers arrived in wagons. They brought tools, seeds, farm animals, guns, and other supplies to help them start farms.

Words To Know

Look at the words below. (Circle) the words you already know. Put a question mark next to the words you don't know.

pioneer

cash crop

*toil

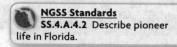
NGSS Standards
SS.4.A.4.2 Describe pioneer life in Florida.

▼ **A pioneer blockhouse in the 1800s**

Library of Congress Prints and Photographs Division Washington - D.C. 20540 USA

Pioneers

NGSS Standards
SS.4.A.4.2 Describe pioneer life in Florida.

After Florida became a U.S. territory, American settlers poured into the area. The new settlers were **pioneers**. A pioneer is the first of non-native people to settle a region. The life of pioneers was often lonely, with few neighbors or roads. They spent most of their time working. Families cleared areas in forests, built simple log cabins, and grew corn and beans. Some farmers only grew crops that they needed to live. Others made money by selling **cash crops**. A cash crop is grown to be sold for profit. Some pioneers suffered attacks by Native Americans during the Seminole wars.

Roles for Men, Women, and Children

Everyone in a pioneer family worked. Men hunted, farmed, raised animals, and built furniture. Women made clothing, tended gardens, cooked meals, and took care of the house. Boys learned to hunt and farm from the men. Girls learned household chores and sewing from the women.

Crackers

Many farmers moved to Florida from the southern foothills of the Appalachian Mountains. Many became cattle ranchers in Florida. In order to move cattle to market, Florida cowboys used dogs and long cow whips. The snap of these whips created a loud "cracking" sound. This sound brought stray cattle back into line. It also earned the cowboys the nickname "crackers." Today, the term "cracker" is sometimes used to identify someone whose family has lived in Florida since the 1800s.

(l) State Archives of Florida, (r) Hulton Archive/Getty Images

Planters

Some of these Florida pioneers were wealthy. They lived on plantations that were like small villages. Plantations often had a flour mill, a blacksmith, and a carpenter's shop. In the center of the plantation was the "big house." That's where the planter's family lived. Male family members helped manage the land and crops. Women and girls took care of the family and organized parties. Plantation families also enslaved many African workers.

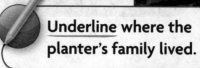

Underline where the planter's family lived.

NGSS Standards
SS.4.A.4.2 Describe pioneer life in Florida.

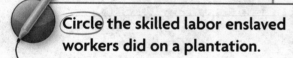

Circle the skilled labor enslaved workers did on a plantation.

Enslaved African Americans

Enslaved workers did most of the work on plantations. Sometimes they worked as carpenters and blacksmiths. But most enslaved workers **toiled** in crop fields. They planted, tended, and harvested crops—mainly cotton. Workdays started at sunup and ended at sundown. Enslaved workers were often treated harshly. They lived in small, poorly made cabins near the fields. Many were not even allowed to learn how to read or write.

Black Seminole

Unlike enslaved African Americans, the Black Seminole were pioneers who lived in freedom. They had escaped slavery and migrated to Florida before it became part of the United States. Like the Seminole, they farmed, hunted, and fished. Over the years, the Black Seminole culture became a mixture of African, Native American, and Spanish traditions. Their language, called Afro-Seminole, used words from African and Native American languages, as well as Spanish and English.

List the different cultures that were part of the Black Seminole.

_____

_____

My Pioneer Daily Schedule

Write a daily schedule of a pioneer child. Be sure to include the time of day for each chore or activity. You will need to draw inferences from this lesson to complete your list.

_____

_____

_____

_____

_____

_____

_____

Jim West/age fotostock

Lesson 3

 Essential Question How do people adapt?

_____

_____

_____

_____

_____

_____

Go back to *Show As You Go!* on pages 80–81.

netw✺rks **There's More Online!** ● Games ● Assessment

Lesson
4 Florida on the Move

? Essential Question

Why do societies change?
What do you think?

_____

_____

_____

_____

_____

_____

Words To Know

Look at the words below.
Circle the words you already
know.

(transportation)

(technology)

(ford)

(*assemble)

NGSS Standards
SS.4.A.4.1 Explain the effects
of technological advances on Florida.

102

Imagine you are an inventor. You need to find a new way of moving people and goods. Your invention should be able to move people and goods quickly and cheaply.

Think about what your invention will look like. Will it travel

on water, on roads, on rails, or in the sky? _Water_

How will it work?

It will be a subway under water. It
will be called the under water ralroad.
It will be at diffrent ralroad stops that
are under water. You will only have to pay 20¢

Why will it be quicker and cheaper than other types of travel?

It will be quicker because there will
be No trafic on land and it is a
subway. It is like a faster bus. Plus
you can see the beautiful coral reef.

Draw your invention in the box below.

Glenn Mitsui/Getty Images

Moving People and Goods

NGSS Standards
SS.4.A.4.1 Explain the effects of technological advances on Florida.

In the early 1800s, the people of Florida needed better **transportation**. Transportation is the way in which people and goods are moved from place to place. Floridians used new **technology** to meet their transportation needs. Technology is the use of skills, ideas, and tools to meet people's needs.

Roads

As more small farmers and plantation owners moved to Florida, more roads were needed to transport their crops to markets. A market is where buyers and sellers exchange goods. At the time Florida became a territory, roads were rough and bumpy. Tree stumps often broke wagons. To fix this problem, people cut logs into flat boards and laid them on the roads. Flat boards made the roads smoother and easier to travel.

Bridges

With road improvements came the building of wooden bridges across rivers. Before roads were improved, river crossings were slow and dangerous. Deep rivers could not be crossed in a wagon, so people would look for a **ford** in the river. A ford is a shallow place where a river or stream may be crossed. Bridges made crossing rivers faster and safer.

> Circle road improvements that were made in the early 1800s.
>
> Underline why bridges were built.

Royalty-Free/CORBIS

▼ **Railroads helped move people and goods.**

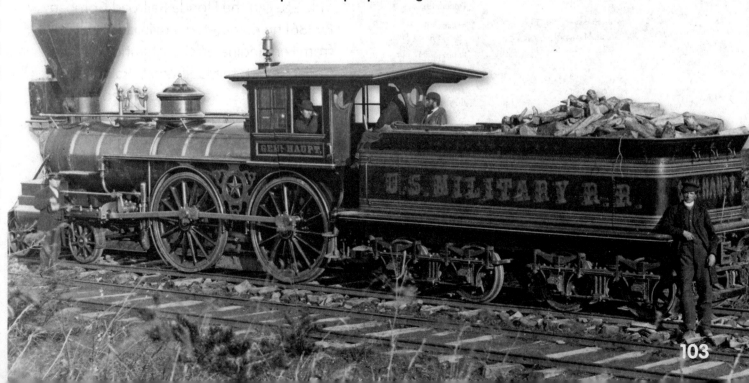

NGSS Standards
SS.4.A.4.1 Explain the effects of technological advances on Florida. **SS.4.A.4.2** Describe pioneer life in Florida. **SS.4.G.1.1** Identify physical features of Florida. **SS.4.G.1.2** Locate and label cultural features on a Florida map. **SS.4.G.1.4** Interpret political and physical maps using map elements (title, compass rose, cardinal directions, intermediate directions, symbols, legend, scale, longitude, latitude)

Boats

Even with new roads and bridges, water travel was still faster than traveling by land. Farmers used sailboats to move their goods along rivers to port cities. Ports are places with at least one harbor. Ships dock at harbors to load or unload people or goods. But sailboats relied on wind, and if there was little wind, they were slow. Was there a way to make boats faster?

A new invention helped! In 1829 the first boat powered by a new technology—the steam engine—arrived in Florida. Steam engine motors are powered by heat. Steam engines allowed boats to move faster. Steamships brought supplies to Florida's pioneers and took loads of cotton and other crops to cities in the North.

Underline the effects steamboats had on people. Circle the effects that railroads had on people.

▼ **Steamboats made travel on water faster.**

Library of Congress · Prints and Photographs Division (LC-USZC2-3031)

Railroads

The steamboat didn't meet all of Florida's transportation needs. In 1837 one of the first railroads arrived. Workers **assembled** train tracks to connect Tallahassee with Port Leon, near St. Marks. For the first time people and goods could be transported quickly from our capital to the Gulf of Mexico. In the 1850s, David Levy Yulee began the Florida Railroad Company. By 1861 he completed a railroad that ran from Fernandina on the Atlantic coast to Cedar Key on the Gulf coast. Railroads created a faster way to move people and products to faraway places. They also brought in many goods that Floridians needed from faraway places.

Florida Railroads and Steamboat Routes, 1850

ATLANTIC OCEAN

Fernandina
Tallahassee
St. Marks
Lake City
Gainesville
Jacksonville
St. Johns River
Palatka
Cedar Key

Gulf of Mexico

N
W   E
S

0   75   150 miles
0   75   150 kilometers

∿ Steamboat Line
++++ Tallahassee Railroad
++++ Florida Railroad
++++ Atlantic and Gulf Central Railroad

Map and Globe Skills

Which railroad connected Fernandina to Cedar Key?

Technology in Early Florida

Fill in the chart with the effects of technological advances in Florida in the early 1800s. Explain what life was like before the technology and what it was like after the technology was used in Florida.

	Before	After
Roadways		
Bridges		
Steam engine		
Steam boat		
Railroads		

Lesson 4

? Essential Question Why do societies change?

_____

_____

_____

_____

Go back to *Show As You Go!* on pages 80–81.

Florida and the Civil War

How does conflict affect people?
What do you think?

_____

_____

_____

_____

_____

_____

Words To Know

Look at the words below. Tell a partner what you know about these words.

*debate

abolitionist

secede

civil war

blockade

*conduct

NGSS Standards
SS.4.G.1.4 Interpret political and physical maps using map elements (title, compass rose, cardinal directions, intermediate directions, symbols, legend, scale, longitude, latitude)

106

People often have different ideas, opinions, or ways of doing things. This can lead to disagreements among people. Explain a time when you disagreed with someone. What happened?

_____

_____

_____

In the 1700s and 1800s, people in the United States disagreed over the issue of slavery. Over time, our nation divided into free and slave states. Free states did not allow slavery. Slave states were states in which slavery was allowed. The map below shows the division of free and slave states in 1860.

Slave and Free States by 1860

CANADA

VT
ME
OR
MN
NH
WI
MA
NY
MI
RI
IA
PA
CT
NJ
TERRITORIES
IL
IN
OH
DE
CA
MO
VA
MD
KY
TN
NC
AR
SC
MS
AL
GA
ATLANTIC
OCEAN
TX
LA
FL
PACIFIC
OCEAN
Gulf of Mexico
MEXICO
0   250   500 miles
0   250   500 kilometers

Free state
Slave state

Map and Globe Skills

1. Circle the slave states that shared a border with free states.

2. Write a number to finish this sentence:

   In 1860 the United States had _____ slave states.

The Struggle Over Slavery

Between 1812 and 1860, a great national **debate** went on over slavery. Many people in the South saw slavery as necessary to their success as farmers. The economy in the Northern states was based on industries that did not depend on slave labor. Many Northerners and some Southerners were **abolitionists**, or people who were against slavery.

Because of this difference, Congress tried to keep a balance of power between slave states and free states. Some people in slave states worried that if there were more free states, slavery would end, and their way of life would disappear. People in free states feared that if there were more slave states, slavery would never end.

To keep a balance in the number of free and slave states, Congress agreed to admit Iowa and Wisconsin as free states. Florida and Texas would be admitted as slave states near the same time. On March 3, 1845, Florida became the 27th state of the United States. This balance of free and slave states continued until 1858. But this balance did not last, and the struggle over slavery did not end.

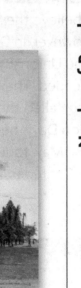

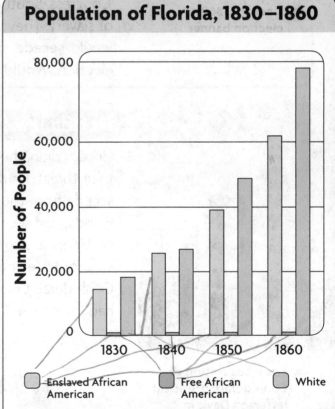

> **Underline** what people in slave states thought would happen if there were more free states than slave states.

▲ The U.S. Capitol is where lawmakers debated the issue of slavery.

Population of Florida, 1830–1860

Number of People (y-axis: 0, 20,000, 40,000, 60,000, 80,000)
(x-axis: 1830, 1840, 1850, 1860)

Enslaved African American | Free African American | White

Chart and Graph Skills

Use a Bar Graph

Which group's population increased the least from 1830 to 1860?

Library of Congress Prints and Photographs Division [LC-USZC2-2032]

107

NGSS Standards
SS.4.A.5.1 Describe Florida's involvement (secession, blockades of ports, the battles of Ft. Pickens, Olustee, Ft. Brooke, Natural Bridge, food supply) in the Civil War.

The Civil War Begins

"A house divided against itself cannot stand. I believe this government cannot endure permanently half slave and half free." This warning was given to the American people by Abraham Lincoln, a candidate for the United States Senate in 1858. Lincoln lost the election, but his warning was right. By 1860 the issue of slavery had torn the country apart.

DID YOU KNOW?

"Union" was a term used in the early 1800s to mean the United States.

The Election of 1860

▲ Lincoln's 1860 election banner

Lincoln lost his race to become a senator in 1858. But because he spoke out against the spread of slavery, Lincoln became popular with people in the North who agreed with him. In 1860 Lincoln ran for President. He promised that if he won, no new slave states would be allowed to join the Union. This meant that the South would lose its power in Congress. Southern lawmakers feared Lincoln would get rid of slavery. They warned that if Lincoln became President, they would **secede**, or withdraw, from the Union. Lincoln won the election. Would states carry out their threat?

Florida Joins the Confederacy

Lincoln didn't believe the Southern states would act on their threat. However, in December 1860, South Carolina did secede from the Union. By February, six more states, including Florida, had seceded. They established the Confederate States of America, also called the Confederacy. Mississippi senator Jefferson Davis became president of the Confederacy. By May, four more Southern states had joined the Confederacy.

▲ The inauguration of Confederate president Jefferson Davis in Montgomery, Alabama.

Draw a box around the name of the president of the Confederacy.

Reading Skill

Draw Inferences

Why did plantation owners fear the election of Abraham Lincoln would threaten their way of life?

_____

_____

_____

108

(t), (r), Library of Congress, (b) Matthew Trommer/age Fotostock

Battle of Fort Sumter

At the time the Confederacy formed, Union troops were in control of some forts in Confederate states. On April 11, 1861, the Confederacy demanded that the Union give up Fort Sumter in South Carolina. The Union refused. After 34 hours of fighting, Union forces surrendered. This attack began the Civil War. A **civil war** is a war among people who live in the same country. People on both sides joined the fight. Most soldiers in Florida fought for the Confederacy, while some left Florida to fight for the Union.

Library of Congress

Battle of Fort Pickens

On October 9, 1861, Confederate troops in Pensacola tried to capture Union-occupied Fort Pickens on Santa Rosa Island. After midnight, 1,200 Confederate troops met Union troops at the fort, but then they backed off. They hoped the Union troops would leave the protection of the fort and attack them in the open. This would leave the Union troops open and easier to attack. However, more Union troops arrived at the island, forcing the Confederates to return to the mainland.

Reading Skill

Compare and Contrast Primary Sources with Secondary Sources

Read the message about the Battle of Fort Sumter from Confederate Brigadier-General G. T. Beauregard to Union Major Robert Anderson, April 11, 1861.

> I am ordered by the Government of the Confederate States to demand the [leaving of troops] of Fort Sumter. . . .
> The flag which you have upheld so long and with so much [courage], under the most trying [conditions], may be saluted by you on taking it down. Colonel Chesnut and Captain Lee will for a reasonable time, await your answer.

1. How is the primary source above similar to the paragraph on this page?

_____

_____

2. How are they different?

_____

_____

NGSS Standards
SS.4.A.1.1 Analyze primary and secondary resources to identify significant individuals and events throughout Florida history.

109

NGSS Standards
SS.4.A.5.1 Describe Florida's involvement (secession, blockades of ports, the battles of Ft. Pickens, Olustee, Ft. Brooke, Natural Bridge, food supply) in the Civil War.

The War Continues

Florida was involved in the Civil War in many ways. As you have read, Floridians fought on both sides. Several small battles took place in Florida. Many Floridians also contributed to the war effort. Read below to find out about Florida's involvement in the Civil War.

Food Supply

Supplies of beef, pork, citrus fruit, salt, grain, and vegetables from Florida farms fed the Confederate Army. In fact, Florida provided so much food to Southern soldiers that the state soon won a special nickname—"the breadbasket of the Confederacy."

The Union Blockade

Union leaders wanted to stop the flow of supplies from Florida to Confederate forces. They also wanted to stop Florida from sending cotton to Europe in exchange for weapons. So the Union Navy began a **blockade** of Florida ports. A blockade is the shutting off of an area to keep people and supplies from going in and out. The Union did this by taking control of ports and watching the Florida coast for Confederate boats. This blockade was **conducted** well. However, some Confederate sailors were able to sneak cotton to Cuba and the Bahamas. They returned with guns, bullets, and medicine to supply the Confederacy.

Underline why Florida was known as the "breadbasket of the Confederacy." Circle why the Union set up a blockade of Florida ports.

Battle of Fort Brooke

Look at the map on this page. One place where Confederate troops were successful in breaking the Union blockade was near Fort Brooke. In response, the Union planned to capture boats used to run supplies in and out of Florida. Union forces fired on Fort Brooke in October 1863. As Confederate troops fired back, Union troops snuck to a river nearby and destroyed several boats. The loss of these boats limited the amount of goods Confederate sailors could sneak in and out of Florida.

Battle of Olustee

In February 1864, the largest battle in Florida took place near the town of Olustee. A force of 5,500 Union soldiers tried to destroy a railroad bridge over the Suwannee River. They wanted to stop the railroad from supplying Confederate troops north of Florida. The Union soldiers were met by 5,000 Confederate troops. For six hours, the two armies were locked in battle among the pines near Olustee. As the smoke began to clear in the early evening, the Union troops retreated east to Jacksonville. Confederate troops saved the railroad bridge from destruction.

The Civil War in Florida

Circle the battle that took place nearest to our state capital.

NGSS Standards
SS.4.A.5.1 Describe Florida's involvement (secession, blockades of ports, the battles of Ft. Pickens, Olustee, Ft. Brooke, Natural Bridge, food supply) in the Civil War. **SS.4.G.1.4** Interpret political and physical maps using map elements (title, compass rose, cardinal directions, intermediate directions, symbols, legend, scale, longitude, latitude)

Reading Skill

Compare and Contrast

Compare and contrast the Battle of Fort Brooke and the Battle of Olustee.

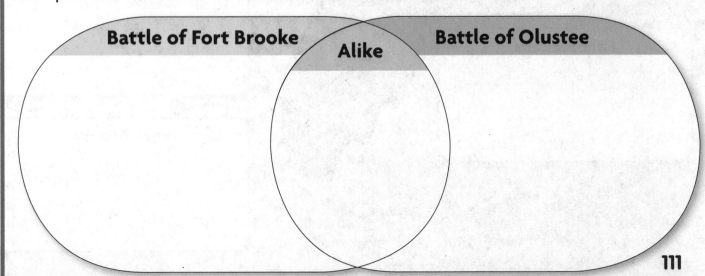

Battle of Fort Brooke   **Alike**   **Battle of Olustee**

Battle of Natural Bridge

The last battle fought in Florida was the Battle of Natural Bridge. In March 1865, Union troops tried to capture Florida's capital, Tallahassee. Union troops headed up the St. Marks River. Confederate gunfire prevented Union soldiers from crossing a natural bridge above the river. A natural bridge is a rock formation that connects two pieces of land to form a bridge. The Confederate victory made Tallahassee the only Confederate capital east of the Mississippi River that the Union Army did not capture.

(Circle) what Union troops were trying to capture during the Battle of Natural Bridge.

A reenactment of the Battle of Natural Bridge ▶

Natural Bridge Battlefield Historic State Park

Fill in the boxes with a description of what happened at each battle and why it was important.

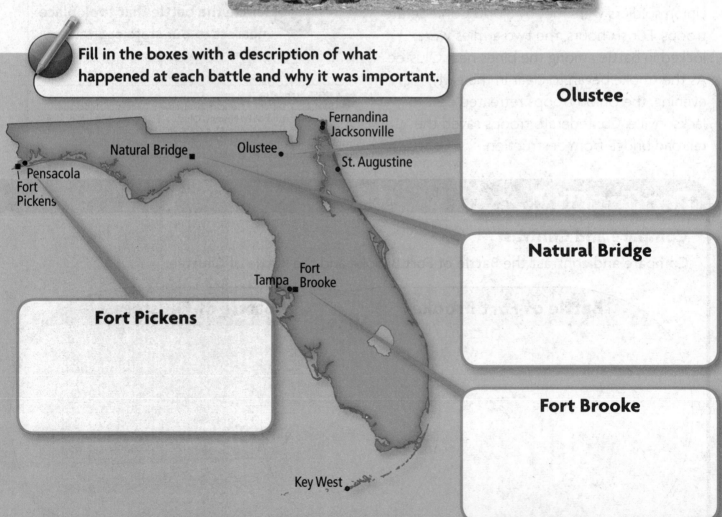

Olustee

Natural Bridge

Fort Brooke

Fort Pickens

Fernandina
Jacksonville
Olustee
St. Augustine
Natural Bridge
Pensacola
Fort Pickens
Fort Brooke
Tampa
Key West

The South Surrenders

Although Florida's troops were able to defend their capital, the Confederacy was losing the war. The Union had more people, more factories, and more money. In April 1865, Confederate general Robert E. Lee surrendered to Union general Ulysses S. Grant. This ended the war. Less than a week after Lee's surrender, Lincoln was shot while watching a play in Washington, D.C. He died the next day.

Robert E. Lee surrendered to Ulysses S. Grant at Appomattox Court House in Virginia. ▶

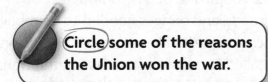

(Circle) some of the reasons the Union won the war.

Lesson 5

 Essential Question **How does conflict affect people?**

_____

_____

_____

_____

_____

_____

Go back to _Show As You Go!_ on pages 80–81. ◀◀◀

networks
There's More Online!
• Games • Assessment

Lesson 6 — Reconstruction in Florida

? Essential Question

Why do societies change?
What do you think?

_____

_____

_____

_____

_____

_____

_____

_____

Words To Know

Look at the words below. Tell a partner what you already know about these words.

black codes

*argue

constitution

sharecropping

segregation

NGSS Standards
SS.4.A.5.2 Summarize challenges Floridians faced during Reconstruction.

114

Challenges are difficulties that make you think, work, or try hard. Think of a challenge in your life. Explain how you met, or overcame, your challenge.

_____

_____

_____

After the Civil War, Floridians faced many challenges. Florida's economy was in ruins. People needed help finding food and shelter. Buildings, railroads, and bridges needed to be rebuilt. Other states were facing these challenges, too. This time in our nation's history was called Reconstruction. During this period, Congress passed laws that would help to rebuild the country and bring the Southern states back into the Union.

Royalty-Free/CORBIS

Underline how the Freedmen's Bureau helped African Americans and poor whites during Reconstruction.

◄ A Freedmen's Bureau school

Rebuilding the South

Rebuilding the country had begun even before the war ended. In January 1865, Congress passed a law that banned slavery throughout the United States. At that time, Congress also knew that many people would need help when the war ended. In March 1865, Congress created a new government agency to help people. This agency was called the Freedmen's Bureau.

The Freedmen's Bureau provided food, shelter, medical care, and schools for freed African Americans and poor whites in the South. In Florida the Freedmen's Bureau ran 87 schools. Church groups in the North sent teachers and money to help support these schools.

NGSS Standards
SS.4.A.5.2 Summarize challenges Floridians faced during Reconstruction.

Many buildings in the South were destroyed during the Civil War. ▼

Reading Skill

Draw Inferences

Why were schools important to the South's recovery after the war?

_____

_____

_____

_____

_____

_____

_____

115

NGSS Standards
SS.4.A.5.2 Summarize challenges Floridians faced during Reconstruction.

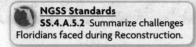

▲ Jonathan Clarkson Gibbs

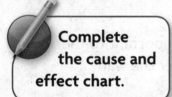

Complete the cause and effect chart.

Expanding Rights

Even though slavery had ended, many white Southerners, including some Floridians, did not want African Americans to have the same rights as whites. Southern states passed laws, called **black codes**, that restricted the rights of African Americans. They were not allowed to own land or to choose where they lived or what jobs they did.

Many people in Congress **argued** against the black codes. In 1868 the United States approved a law. It gave citizenship and the same legal rights as whites to African Americans. These rights included the right to vote for African American men. (At this time, women and Native Americans were still not allowed to vote.)

Congress then required that all Confederate states write new **constitutions** that recognized the rights of African Americans. A constitution is a plan for government. In 1868 Florida voters approved a new constitution. As a result, Florida could rejoin the United States. The new constitution also brought an end to black codes. The Freedmen's Bureau helped African Americans register to vote.

In the election of 1868, many African Americans were elected to office. Jonathan Clarkson Gibbs became Florida's first African American Secretary of State. But Florida, along with other Southern states, found new ways to keep African Americans from voting. In response, in 1870 Congress approved a law to protect the right to vote.

State Archives of Florida

Cause	Effect
Many people in Congress argued that black codes were wrong.	
	Congress allowed Florida to rejoin the United States.
	In 1870 the United States approved a law to protect the right to vote.

Sharecropping

By 1868 African Americans had the right to vote, hold office, and hold jobs. Yet many African Americans were poor. Many of those living in Florida knew how to farm but did not own land or homes.

White farmers still owned most of the farmland. But they had little or no money to pay freedmen or poor whites to work the land. So they rented their land and usually accepted part of the crops grown on it as rent. The landowner's share could be as much as half of the crops. Renting land for a share of the crops grown on it is called **sharecropping**. People who worked this land were called sharecroppers.

Many freed African Americans got jobs and homes as sharecroppers. Some poor whites who did not own land also worked as sharecroppers. Many of these poor whites were farmers whose homes were destroyed during the war. They lost their land when they could not repay loans they had taken out to rebuild.

Sharecropping was a hard life. Sharecroppers often had to borrow money to buy seeds and supplies. Crops were often poor, and prices were low. Each year most sharecroppers slipped deeper into debt.

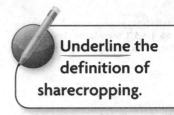

Underline the definition of sharecropping.

(bkgd) Photo by Lynn Betts, USDA Natural Resources Conservation, (m) Library of Congress

Reading Skill

Summarize

Summarize the challenges sharecroppers faced.

_____

_____

_____

_____

_____

_____

Based on what you read about sharecropping, write a caption for the photograph above.

_____

NGSS Standards
SS.4.A.5.2 Summarize challenges Floridians faced during Reconstruction.

117

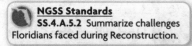
NGSS Standards
SS.4.A.5.2 Summarize challenges Floridians faced during Reconstruction.

The End of Reconstruction

The rights gained by African Americans during Reconstruction angered many white Floridians. Some joined secret groups, like the Ku Klux Klan. This group often terrorized and sometimes killed African Americans.

In 1877 the United States ended Reconstruction. The Southern states then passed Jim Crow laws. These laws made the **segregation** of African Americans and whites legal. Segregation is the separation of people based on race. Under Jim Crow laws, African Americans could not use the same schools, restaurants, hotels, or water fountains as whites. They had to sit in the back of trains, and their schools received little or no money for supplies.

Other laws required people to pay a special tax, called a poll tax, if they wanted to vote. Many African Americans could not afford to pay this tax. As a result, many African Americans no longer voted.

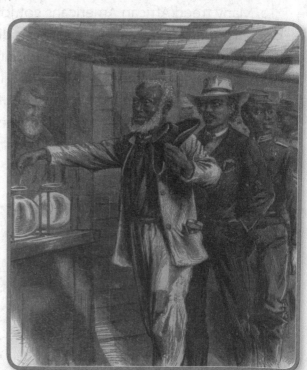

A woodcut of African Americans voting for the first time. ▶

Library of Congress

THINK • PAIR • SHARE
Think about what you have learned in this lesson. Choose a challenge Floridians faced during Reconstruction, such as segregation or sharecropping. Find a partner and share your ideas. Then share your ideas with your class.

Reading Skill

Draw Inferences

What effect did poll taxes have on African Americans?

_____

_____

_____

Reconstruction in Florida

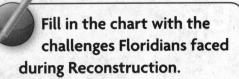
Fill in the chart with the challenges Floridians faced during Reconstruction.

```
┌─────────────────────────┐        ┌─────────────────────────┐
│                         │        │                         │
│                         │        │                         │
│                         │        │                         │
└─────────────────────────┘        └─────────────────────────┘
              ┌──────────────────────┐
              │   Reconstruction     │
              │     Challenges       │
              └──────────────────────┘
┌─────────────────────────┐        ┌─────────────────────────┐
│                         │        │                         │
│                         │        │                         │
│                         │        │                         │
└─────────────────────────┘        └─────────────────────────┘
```

Lesson 6

 Essential Question Why do societies change?

_____

_____

_____

_____

_____

Go back to *Show As You Go!* on pages 80–81.

Florida's Early History

Read the words in the box and the speech bubbles below. Decide which person from Florida's early history would have made each statement. Write the name of the person's group below the speech bubble.

Black Seminole	**Cracker**	**enslaved African American**
abolitionist	**pioneer**	**sharecropper**

I built a log cabin for my family to live in. I also farmed the land.

I rented the land that I farmed and paid my rent with some of my crop.

I migrated from the foothills of the Appalachian Mountains. In Florida I raised cattle.

I escaped slavery, and Native Americans helped me live in Florida.

I fought for enslaved people to be free.

I lived on a plantation and had to pick cotton for no money.

Unit Project

A museum has hired you and a partner to create an exhibit about an event in the early history of Florida. Make an exhibit on one of the events you learned about in this unit. Before you begin working, look back at **Show as You Go!** on pages 80–81 to review your notes. Read the list below to see what information should be included in your museum exhibit. As you work, check off each item as you include it.

When General Andrew Jackson won the First Seminole War, he told the Spanish Governor, "your personal rights and private property shall be respected."

Your museum exhibit should...   Yes, it does!

include text that describes what happened during the event and why the event was important. ☐

include at least one image that supports your text. ☐

include research from primary sources. ☐

include research from secondary sources. ☐

be neat and legible. ☐

be interesting to look at and appealing to visitors. ☐

Think about the Big Idea

BIG IDEA Conflict causes change.

What did you learn in this unit that helps you understand the BIG IDEA?

_____

_____

_____

Read the passage "Steam Engines" and then answer Numbers 1 and 2.

Steam Engines

1 THE history of the invention of the steam engine started a long time ago. A man named Hero of Alexandria, who lived in ancient Egypt, was the first person to experiment with a steam engine. In the early 1700s, Thomas Newcomen made the first useful steam engine in England. In 1765 James Watt made important improvements to the steam engine.

2 By the early 1800s, steam engines were being used in the United States. The first steam engine was used in Florida in 1827. It might not seem like it now, but the steam engine was a very important invention. For one thing, the steam engine changed transportation. Before the steam engine, people used sailboats, animals, or walked to get from place to place.

going from pla

3 The steam engine created new, faster modes of transportation for people and goods. For instance, boats powered by steam engines, called steamboats, traveled faster than sailboats could. Steamboats had another advantage over sailboats too. Steamboats didn't have to rely on the wind to move people and goods.

4 Steam engines also helped the development of another important form of transportation—railroads. Steam engines powered trains as they moved across land. Unlike steamboats, railroads could reach inland places that weren't located along the coasts. Now moving people and goods across land became easier and faster.

"*Steam Engines*" property of McGraw-Hill Education.

GO ON →

Now answer Numbers 1 and 2. Base your answers on the passage "Steam Engines."

1 This question has two parts. First, answer Part A. Then, answer Part B.

Part A What was the effect of the steam engine on people's lives?

Ⓐ The steam engine made people in Florida rich. ✗

Ⓑ The steam engine made transportation faster and easier. —

Ⓒ The steam engine used windpower to help people travel. ✗

Ⓓ The steam engine powered household appliances. ✗

Part B Which sentence from the passage supports the answer in Part A?

Ⓐ "The history of the invention of the steam engine started a long time ago. "

Ⓑ "It might not seem like it now, but the steam engine was a very important invention."

Ⓒ "The steam engine created new, faster modes of transportation for people and goods."

Ⓓ "Steamboats didn't have to rely on the wind to move people and goods."

2 How are steamboats different from trains?

Ⓐ Steamboats move faster than trains. ✗

Ⓑ Steamboats and trains use steam engines. ✗

Ⓒ Steamboats travel on water and trains travel on land.

Ⓓ Steamboats and trains were invented by different people. ✗

GO ONLINE to connected.mcgraw-hill.com for enhanced
Florida Test Preparation options, available through Engrade.

123

UNIT 4

Florida in Modern Times

 BIG IDEA Change happens over time.

After the Civil War, Florida began to change. Why did these changes happen? What caused them to happen? In this unit, you will read about the changes that came to Florida and why they happened. You will learn how these changes made Florida a modern state. As you read, think about how change happens over time.

Lesson 1

Cause

Effect

Lesson 2

Cause

Effect

 **networks**

There's More Online!
● Skill Builders
● Vocabulary Flashcards

Show As You Go! After you read each lesson in this unit, use these pages to record an important cause and effect that you learned about in each lesson. You will use your notes to help you complete a project at the end of the unit.

Lesson 3

Cause

Effect

Lesson 5

Cause

Effect

Lesson 4

Cause

Effect

Lesson 6

Cause

Effect

Reading Skill

NGSS Standards

LAFS.4.RI.3.9 Integrate information from two texts on the same topic in order to write or speak about the subject knowledgeably.

SS.4.A.1.2 Synthesize information related to Florida history through print and electronic media.

Integrate Information

To integrate means to synthesize, or bring together. When you integrate and synthesize, you take information from a source and combine it with information from another source. You integrate information all the time. For example, before school you might see a weather report saying that today will be hot. Then your family reminds you that you have a soccer game after school. And so, you grab a bottle of water because you have integrated two different sources of information. You can integrate information from different texts too.

LEARN IT

To integrate information from two texts:

- Read the passages to find out what the topic is.

- Read carefully to see the different things each passage says about the same topic.

> This sentence states the topic.

Encyclopedia: Thomas Alva Edison born on February 11, 1847, in Milan, Ohio. He died October 18, 1931, in West Orange, New Jersey. Edison was an American inventor known for introducing the world to the modern age of electricity. From his laboratories came the phonograph, the light bulb, parts for a movie-making machine, and many other inventions.

Web site: Thomas Edison was born in 1847 in Ohio. As a child, he was curious about everything and loved to learn. When he grew up he became an inventor. He made many things, including an alkaline storage battery, and several smaller inventions that paved the way for things we know today, such as television, movie theaters, and MP3 players.

> This information is not in the second passage.

◀ Thomas Edison

Library of Congress

TRY IT

You can use a graphic organizer to help you integrate information.
Fill in the chart with the information from the paragraphs on page 126.

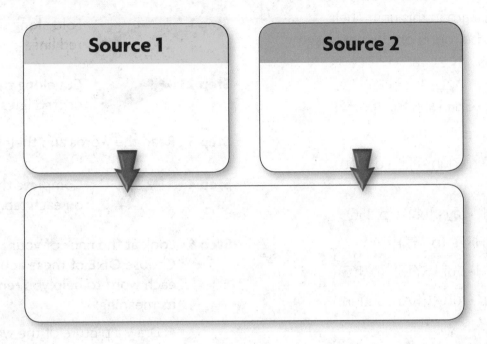

Source 1	Source 2

APPLY IT

- Read the passages below. Then circle the topic and underline the different information each passage contains.

Newspaper: The hurricane of 1926 caused devastation as it hit the Miami coast. A storm surge of 15 feet was reported at Coconut Grove. Most of downtown Miami was destroyed.

Journal: My family hid in the house as the hurricane hit. The walls shook so hard I thought they would fall down. After it was over, we inspected the damage outside. Everything was wet. It looked as if the neighborhood had been washed away.

- Integrate and synthesize the passages and write this information on the lines.

Words to Know

NGSS Standards
LAFS.4.RI.2.4 Determine the meaning of general academic and domain-specific words or phrases in a text relevant to a grade 4 topic or subject area.

The list below shows some important words you will learn in this unit. Their definitions can be found on the next page. Read the words.

recession (rih • SEH • shuhn) (p. 132)

industry (IHN • duhs • tree) (p. 133)

independent (in • duh • PEN • duhnt) (p. 141)

dictator (DIHK • tay • tuhr) (p. 156)

enlist (ihn • LIHST) (p. 157)

civil rights (SIH • vuhl RYTS) (p. 163)

integration (in • tuh • GRAY • shuhn) (p. 163)

boycott (BOI • kaht) (p. 166)

FOLDABLES®

The **Foldable** on the next page will help you learn these important words. Follow the steps below to make your Foldable.

Step 1 Fold along the solid red line.

Step 2 Cut along the dotted lines.

Step 3 Read the words and their definitions.

Step 4 Complete the activities on each tab.

Step 5 Look at the back of your Foldable. Choose ONE of these activities for each word to help you remember its meaning:

- Draw a picture of the word.
- Write a description of the word.
- Write how the word is related to something you know.

◀ **The Ponce de León hotel in St. Augustine**

Courtesy of the State Archives of Florida

A **recession** is a period of slow economic activity.	Write a synonym and antonym for the word *recession*.
An **industry** is all the businesses that make one kind of product or provide one kind of service.	List two examples of industries.
Independence is another word for freedom.	List other words that you think of when you think of *independence*.
A **dictator** is a person who rules a country alone.	Write the root word of *dictator* and explain what it means.
To **enlist** means to volunteer for military service.	*Enlisting* means volunteering. What does it mean to volunteer for something?
Civil rights are the rights of every citizen to be treated equally under the law.	Write a sentence using *civil rights*.
Integration is the act of making something open to people of all ethnic groups.	Change the suffix of the word *integration* and write two examples of what you come up with.
To **boycott** is to refuse to do business with a person, group, company, or country.	Why would you decide to boycott a company?

recession

recession

CUT HERE

industry

industry

independence

independence

dictator

dictator

enlist

enlist

civil rights

civil rights

integration

integration

boycott

boycott

NGSS Standards
SS.4.A.1.1 Analyze primary and secondary sources to identify significant individuals and events throughout Florida history.

Time Lines

A time line is a type of secondary source. Remember that a secondary source is a source written or made after an event happened. A time line is a diagram that shows the order of events in history. The date at the farthest left is the oldest date on the time line. The date on the farthest right is the most recent date. Time lines can show us when events took place in relation to each other.

 Document-Based Questions

Read the time line. This time line is divided into 10-year segments. As you read, complete the following activities.

1. **How many years come between the first event and the last event on the time line?**

   _____

2. Circle the date when Reconstruction ended.

3. Put a box around events that only affected Florida.

4. **What does the time line tell you about how life changed in Florida during these years?**

   _____

   _____

▲ James Weldon Johnson

network's
There's More Online!
● Skill Builders
● Resource Library

Courtesy of the State Archives of Florida

1900
James Weldon Johnson helps write the words and music to "Lift Ev'ry Voice and Sing."

1865
End of Civil War

1877
End of Reconstruction

| 1870 | 1880 | 1890 | 1900 |

1885
A new state constitution is written for Florida.

1891
The Tampa Bay Hotel opens.

Florida Grows

? Essential Question

**Why do societies change?
What do you think?**

_____

_____

_____

_____

_____

_____

_____

Have you ever arrived home from school and noticed that something had changed? How did that make you feel? Did you like the changes or not? Write your thoughts below.

_____

_____

_____

The end of the Civil War and Reconstruction brought many changes to Florida. The freeing of enslaved people and the cost of the war had left many Southern states in a **recession**. A recession is a period of slow economic activity. In this lesson, you will learn how Florida recovered from the post-Civil War recession.

THINK • PAIR • SHARE

Why do you think the freeing of enslaved people contributed to the recession? Find a partner and share your ideas.

The Ponce de León hotel in St. Augustine was built in the late 1800s to attract wealthy tourists. ▼

Words To Know

Write what you think these words mean on the lines.

recession _____

industry _____

immigrant _____

entrepreneur _____

*according _____

NGSS Standards
SS.4.A.4.1 Explain the effects of technological advances on Florida. **SS.4.A.6.1** Describe the economic development of Florida's major industries.

▲ Trains like this one helped Florida grow.

The Growth of Industry

Unlike many of the other Southern states, Florida didn't depend totally on cotton. Florida's economy relied on many other **industries** as well. An industry is all the businesses that make one kind of product or provide one kind of service. Important industries in Florida included phosphate, timber, cattle, citrus, and cigars.

In the 1880s, phosphate was discovered in Florida near Peace River. Phosphate is a mineral that occurs naturally in the ground. After it is mined from the earth, phosphate is used in fertilizer and cattle feed. Phosphate deposits were soon found in other parts of Florida. The mining of this mineral quickly turned into a valuable business. Florida became a major world supplier of phosphate.

The growth of railroads in Florida helped phosphate and other industries expand. Railroads made transporting goods faster and easier, which helped businesses make money.

▲ A train loaded with phosphate

How did railroads help the growth of Florida's industries?

133

NGSS Standards
SS.4.A.6.1 Describe the economic development of Florida's major industries.
SS.4.G.1.4 Interpret political and physical maps using map elements (title, compass rose, cardinal directions, intermediate directions, symbols, legend, scale, longitude, latitude).

Other Industries

Phosphate was just one of the many industries that grew when railroads expanded. Other industries included cattle ranching, citrus, cigars, and timber. Timber refers to trees and the process of using the wood from trees to make many different products. These other industries provided Floridians with new jobs and new ways to be proud of their state.

Royalty-Free/CORBIS

Timber

Northwest Florida, some of the central parts of the state, and much of the northeast coast of Florida have abundant forests. The wood from these trees was used for building masts on ships and for building houses. Pine trees provided sap that was used to make turpentine, an ingredient in paint thinner. Later, trees were also used to make pencils. Wood from Florida trees was shipped into the northern part of the United States and even as far away as Europe!

Cattle

Organized cattle ranching in Florida began in 1565 when the Spanish brought the first cattle to the area. Do you remember that the Spanish and Native Americans raised cows on missions? Florida also supplied a lot of beef for the Confederate Army during the Civil War. After the war, Florida continued to ship cattle all over the country. Over time, cattle ranching became an important business in Florida.

Florida Industries, Late 1800s

Map and Globe Skills

1. Look at where citrus is grown in Florida. Why do you think citrus is grown here?

_____

2. Why is the timber industry more active in northern Florida?

_____

NGSS Standards
SS.4.A.6.1 Describe the economic development of Florida's major industries. **SS.4.A.6.3** Describe the contributions of significant individuals to Florida.

◀ **Lue Gim Gong**

Citrus

Like the cattle industry, the citrus industry has been in Florida since 1565. The Spanish planted the first orange trees when St. Augustine was founded. In the late 1800s, demand for oranges and grapefruits grew. As a result, farmers planted more and more trees. By the end of the 1800s, Florida citrus was being shipped all over the United States and even to Europe. A man named Lue Gim Gong helped meet this demand. Gong was a Chinese **immigrant**. An immigrant is a person who lives in a country in which he or she was not born. Gong knew a lot about plants. He developed cold-resistant grapefruits and oranges. The types of citrus fruits that Gong developed are still grown in Florida today. His kinds of fruits enabled farmers to sell more crops.

Courtesy of the State Archives of Florida

Cigars

Tobacco had been grown in Florida since before the Civil War. Florida's climate, like that of many Southern states, was ideal for growing tobacco. In the late 1800s, cigar manufacturers began moving to Florida to set up new businesses. Factories sprang up in Key West and Tampa. These factories hired hundreds of workers to roll tobacco leaves and sort cigars. These cigars were shipped by railroad all over the United States.

Reading Skill

Sequencing

Pick one of the industries you've read about on these pages. In the boxes below, draw three scenes that show how that industry developed in Florida.

Henry Plant ▼

Henry Flagler ▼

Julia Tuttle ▼

Railroads Reach Across Florida

In 1881 only 550 miles of railroad existed in the whole state. None of these railroads were in southern Florida. Only 19 years later, more than 3,500 miles of railroad covered the entire state. How did this big change happen? Read on to find out.

Henry Plant

One wealthy businessman, Henry Plant, was very important to the growth of Florida railroads. Plant built a railroad that joined Jacksonville on the east coast to Tampa on the west coast. This was important because both of these cities were port cities, meaning they had a lot of trade coming in by boat. Now these trade goods could travel quickly across the state. This railroad also helped the development of the citrus industry. It gave farmers quicker and cheaper options to sell their crops in Northern markets. Plant also built the Tampa Bay Hotel, which attracted tourists to the area.

Henry Flagler

Like Plant, Henry Flagler was a wealthy **entrepreneur** who built railroads in Florida. An entrepreneur is a person who starts and owns a business. Flagler, frustrated by the lack of good hotels, built the Ponce de León hotel in St. Augustine. To help tourists get to his hotel, he built a railroad from Jacksonville to St. Augustine. Later, he extended this railroad line to reach West Palm Beach.

NGSS Standards
SS.4.A.4.1 Explain the effects of technological advances on Florida. **SS.4.A.6.3** Describe the contributions of significant individuals to Florida. **SS.4.E.1.1** Identify entrepreneurs from various social and ethnic backgrounds who have influenced Florida and local economy.

Why did Henry Flagler decide to build a railroad to St. Augustine?

_____

_____

Then something happened that caused Flagler to extend his railroads even farther south. A bad freeze in the winter of 1894–1895 damaged citrus crops. Flagler, who earned money when farmers used his trains to ship their fruit, was upset.

According to a story, Julia Tuttle, who lived in Miami, sent Flagler an orange blossom as proof that the frost hadn't reached that far south. This convinced Flagler that building a railroad to reach citrus fields around Miami would make him money. Flagler built the first railroad to Miami in 1896.

One of Flagler's most famous feats, however, was building a railroad bridge from the mainland to Key West. This bridge extended over 128 miles of water and the islands of the Keys. For the first time, Key West was connected to the rest of the state.

The railroads in Florida connected cities and towns across the undeveloped parts of the state. Railroads allowed smaller towns to build up their farms. They also helped industries grow and made delivering the mail faster. They helped tourists get to the hotels that Plant and Flagler built. Without railroads, the southern parts of Florida might have remained undeveloped for a long time. Thanks to Henry Plant and Henry Flagler, however, more and more of Florida opened up to the world.

DID YOU KNOW?
After the railroad to Miami was built, Miami residents wanted to change the name of their town to Flagler, but he politely turned them down.

On the last page, underline the contributions that Henry Plant made to Florida.

NGSS Standards
SS.4.A.4.1 Explain the effects of technological advances on Florida.
SS.4.G.1.4 Interpret political and physical maps using map elements (title, compass rose, cardinal directions, intermediate directions, symbols, legend, scale, longitude, latitude).

Florida Railroads, 1880–1900

136-137 (bkgs) Ingram Publishing / age Fotostock

Tallahassee
Jacksonville
Gainesville
St. Augustine
Ocala
Cedar Key
ATLANTIC OCEAN
Titusville
Orlando
Gulf of Mexico
Kissimmee
Tampa
Arcadia
Lake Okeechobee
West Palm Beach
Miami
Key West

0   100   200 miles
0   100   200 kilometers

— Railroads in 1880
— Railroads in 1900

N W E S

Map and Globe Skills

1. Circle the southernmost point people could reach by 1880.

2. Put a box around the most southern point of the railroads in 1900.

3. Use the map scale. How much farther south did a railroad go in 1900 than in 1880?

On the lines below, make a list that summarizes the contributions that immigrants made to Florida.

_____

_____

_____

_____

_____

New Faces

Florida grew in other ways too. After the recession ended, more and more immigrants came to Florida. They came for many reasons. Some were escaping hard times in their home countries. Others came looking for work or for freedom.

When you and your family go out to dinner, you are able to choose between sushi, spaghetti, burritos, and many other foods. You have these choices because of immigrants. When immigrants moved to Florida, they brought the foods from their home countries with them. They also brought their languages and customs. For example, many immigrants spoke Spanish, Italian, or Greek. These different languages gave us words that we now use all the time in English. For example, do you like spaghetti? *Spaghetti* is an Italian word.

Once in the United States, immigrants continued to follow some of the customs of their home countries. These customs included celebrating festivals and holidays, playing music, and wearing special clothing. Even dancing was a way to preserve and remember the customs of their home countries.

Immigrants of all ages came to Florida from all over the world. ▼

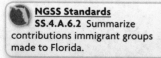

NGSS Standards
SS.4.A.6.2 Summarize contributions immigrant groups made to Florida.

From the photos below, pick a person you learned about in this lesson, and write a mini biography of him or her. Explain how this person made contributions to Florida. (Circle) the picture of the person you choose.

Name: _____

What he or she is known for: _____

_____

_____

Lesson 1

? **Essential Question** Why do societies change?

_____

_____

_____

Go back to _Show As You Go!_ on pages 124–125. ≪

networks
connected.mcgraw-hill.com
● Games ● Assessment

The Spanish American War and Florida

NGSS Standards
SS.4.G.1.4 Interpret political and physical maps using map elements (title, compass rose, cardinal directions, intermediate directions, symbols, legend, scale, longitude, latitude).

? Essential Question

How does conflict affect people?

What do you think?

_____

_____

_____

_____

_____

Words To Know

Write a number in each box to show how much you know about the meaning of each word.

1 = I have no idea!
2 = I know a little.
3 = I know a lot.

☐ *frequently

☐ independent

☐ mobilize

Neighbors frequently watch out for one another. For example, your family might watch a neighbor's house and pets while your neighbors are gone. The United States watches over its neighbors too. In the late 1800s, the United States was paying special attention to one neighbor in particular—Cuba.

At this time, the United States cared about what happened in Cuba for several reasons. Many Americans lived in Cuba, and many Cuban immigrants lived in Florida. Cuba and the United States were trade partners too. These reasons contributed to the United States becoming involved in a war with Spain, Cuba's ruling country. This war—the Spanish American War—started in April 1898. Read a newspaper account about this war on the following pages.

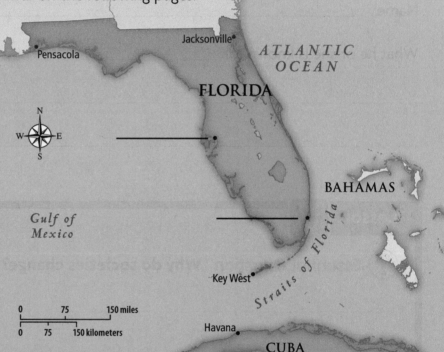

Map and Globe Skills

1. On the map, label the following cities:

- Miami
- Tampa

2. Use the map scale to figure out about how many miles it is from Havana to Key West.

_____

WEATHER

SUNNY
HIGH 72°

Networks News
SINCE 1865

VOL. 79, NO. 137   DECEMBER 10, 1898   PRICE 50¢

SPECIAL EDITION

Florida State Parks

NGSS Standards
SS.4.A.6.4 Describe effects of the Spanish American War on Florida.

▲ Wreckage of the USS *Maine*

BACKGROUND OF THE WAR

Our readers may remember that Cuba had been a Spanish colony since the early 1500s. In the middle of the 1800s, Cubans began to fight against this Spanish rule. Cubans wanted to be **independent**, or free.

Cubans were still fighting Spain for their independence at the beginning of this year, 1898. Many Americans, especially Cubans living here in Florida, supported the independence movement. One of these people was Vincente Martínez Ybor. Read our interview with him on the next page.

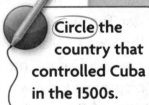

Circle the country that controlled Cuba in the 1500s.

MAINE EXPLOSION

Then, on February 15 of this year, the American ship the USS *Maine* exploded in the harbor of Havana, Cuba. Our country lost 266 sailors in this terrible event. Americans across the country were very angry, and most of them blamed Spain for the explosion. Our country was on the edge of war with Spain.

Networks News special edition continues on the next page.

SPOTLIGHT:
Vincente Martínez Ybor

> Underline how Vincente Martínez Ybor contributed to Florida.

HELPING THE INDEPENDENCE MOVEMENT

Cuban immigrant Vincente Martínez Ybor supported the Cuban independence movement for many years. He came to Florida in the mid 1800s to start a cigar business. Located in Tampa, this business has been very successful and has helped our economy grow. Our reporters sat down with him a couple of years ago.

Question: How did the area around your cigar factory become known as Ybor City?

Ybor: I wanted to make life easier for my workers, so I built places where they could live around the factory. Other businesses started up in the area too. Eventually the area took on my name.

Question: What is life like in Ybor City?

Ybor: It is a diverse place. Cubans, Spaniards, Italians, Germans, Jews, and even a few Chinese immigrants live there. Many of these people work in my factory.

Question: How do you support the Cuban independence movement?

Ybor: I send the movement money whenever I can. I would love to see an independent Cuba. Perhaps Cuba will be free soon, just like the United States.

PREPARING FOR WAR

In April 1898 Congress declared war on Spain, and our country started to **mobilize**, or get ready for war. The military started to train soldiers to fight the Spanish. Many of our cities here in Florida, especially Tampa, became bases for soldiers preparing for the war. In all, reports show that some 30,000 soldiers came to Florida.

These soldiers became new customers for our Florida businesses. As a result, our economy grew. Mobilizing also helped the economy because the military built more harbors along our coasts. These harbors made it easier for the military to ship soldiers to Cuba.

▲ Soldiers training in Tampa

(t) Florida State Parks, (b) Courtesy of the State Archives of Florida

ROUGH RIDERS

By June the United States was ready to attack. On the 10th, American troops landed near Santiago, Cuba, and prepared to take the city. One person involved in this attack was Theodore "Teddy" Roosevelt. He had started a cavalry unit, which is a fighting force made up of soldiers who fight on horseback. Teddy nicknamed his cavalry the "Rough Riders." The Rough Riders were one of the first units ready to fight because they already knew how to ride horses and shoot guns. This unit helped the Americans win an important battle near Santiago.

The Spanish American War ended about a month later, in July 1898. The United States defeated Spain, and Cuba became independent.

▲ **Roosevelt leads the Rough Riders**

EFFECTS OF WAR

The war has changed our state in several ways. The number of businesses and harbors has grown, and officials expect the population of Florida to rise. They think that many soldiers who trained in Florida will decide to live here permanently. Friends and family of these soldiers will also probably come to live in the state.

What effects did the Spanish American War have on Florida?

_____

_____

NGSS Standards
SS.4.A.6.3 Describe the contributions of significant individuals to Florida. **SS.4.A.6.4** Describe effects of the Spanish American War on Florida. **SS.4.E.1.1** Identify entrepreneurs from various social and ethnic backgrounds who have influenced Florida and local economy.

Lesson 2

(?) Essential Question   How does conflict affect people?

_____

_____

_____

Go back to *Show As You Go!* on pages 124–125. «

netw⊙rks   connected.mcgraw-hill.com
● Games ● Assessment

3 Boom and Bust

? Essential Question

Why do societies change?
What do you think?

_____

_____

_____

_____

_____

_____

_____

Words To Know

Look at the words below. Rank them from 1 to 5 based on how much you know about them. Write 1 next to the word that you know the most about.

boom

mass production

*substitute

bust

depression

NGSS Standards
SS.4.A.7.1 Describe the causes and effects of the 1920's Florida land boom and bust.

Have you ever had a growth spurt? During a growth spurt, you might outgrow your clothes quickly. Florida had its own kind of growth spurt following the Spanish American War. The state's population and industries grew quickly, causing an economic boom. A boom is a period of rapid growth.

In the early 1920s, Florida continued to grow. One reason for this was the end of World War I. World War I started in Europe in 1914. At first the United States stayed out of this war. Then, in 1917, the United States entered the war and sent many soldiers to Europe to fight.

When the war ended in 1918 with victory for the Americans and their European allies, Americans felt relieved. They were tired of wartime and wanted life to be fun. As a result, more and more people became interested in traveling and tourism. Florida was one place that appealed to them because of its warm, sunny weather, beautiful beaches, and many hotels. Many of these people bought land in Florida and decided to make the state their permanent home.

Circle the reasons why people came to Florida.

Easier Travel

In the early 1900s, some improvements in transportation made traveling to Florida easier. First, a carmaker named Henry Ford started to use **mass production**. Mass production means making a large number of products quickly. By using mass production, a car factory could produce cars very fast. Producing cars quickly and in large quantities made them cheaper. As a result, more and more people could afford to buy cars. Cars allowed families to travel farther than ever before, and many people visited Florida.

Airplanes also made travel faster. During World War I, many companies in the United States had built airplanes for the war. After the war, some of these companies expanded and began to offer passenger flights. These passenger flights helped increase tourism. In addition, in 1920 a Florida business started to offer international flights from Key West to Havana, Cuba. With both airplanes and cars available, Americans had more reasons than ever to visit Florida.

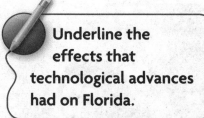

Underline the effects that technological advances had on Florida.

Land Boom

As you have read, cars, airplanes, and railroads brought more and more new people to Florida during the early 1920s. These new people needed places to live and places to buy the things they needed. Entrepreneurs in Florida bought land and built homes, stores, hotels, and other buildings for these new people. Demand for land in Florida was high, so the prices kept rising. This land boom made some people very rich. They bought land at a low price and sold it at a high price for a huge profit.

NGSS Standards
SS.4.A.4.1 Explain the effects of technological advances on Florida. **SS.4.A.7.1** Describe the causes and effects of the 1920's Florida land boom and bust.

Hulton Archive/Getty Images

Resort hotels line the beachside in Florida. ▼

145

Inventing in Florida

You just read about inventions that affected the land boom. Thomas Edison and John Gorrie, two men who lived in Florida during two different time periods, made contributions with their own inventions.

▲ John Gorrie (top) and a replica of his invention (right)

John Gorrie

John Gorrie's invention helped pave the way for the modern air conditioners that we use today. The invention of air conditioning made Florida a more appealing place to live. Most people in Florida learned to live with the heat, but some people moved north when the summer months became too hot.

John Gorrie, a doctor, was worried about his patients in Apalachicola. It was hot in the hospital where he worked, and he wanted to make his patients more comfortable. In 1842 he invented a machine that cooled the air inside the room—one of the first air conditioners! The process of keeping something cool is known as refrigeration. The method that Gorrie developed is still used in today's refrigerators. At the time, not a lot of people thought his invention was useful. Other inventors, though, later expanded on his work to create modern air conditioning. By the early 1920s, air conditioners had been installed in some Florida buildings. Now even during the hot summer months, people could be comfortable indoors. Air conditioning encouraged more people to live in and visit Florida, adding to the land boom.

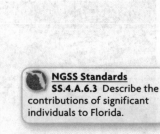

NGSS Standards
SS.4.A.6.3 Describe the contributions of significant individuals to Florida.

Thomas Edison

Thomas Alva Edison invented many things. He is best known for helping invent the light bulb in 1880. He also invented the phonograph in 1877. The phonograph was the first kind of machine to play sound from a recording. Without this invention, you might not be listening to music on your CD or MP3 player today. Edison's inventions made life easier and more fun for all Americans.

In the late 1800s, Edison visited Florida and loved its sunny weather. He decided to build a house and laboratory in Fort Myers. Edison's family lived in Florida for many months during the year throughout the early 1900s. During his time in Florida, Edison helped the navy. He worked hard on many experiments at a naval base in Key West. He worked on submarines, making communications better. He improved the periscope, a tube-like device that helped sailors see above water. Edison also worked on **substitutes** for dyes, medicine, and other items.

"Genius is one per cent inspiration, [and] ninety-nine per cent perspiration." – **Thomas Edison**

perspiration sweat

What do you think this quote means?

_____

_____

Write three facts about each inventor's contributions to Florida.

Facts to Know	
Gorrie	**Edison**
•	•
•	•
•	•

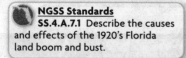

NGSS Standards
SS.4.A.7.1 Describe the causes and effects of the 1920's Florida land boom and bust.

Good Times Fade

As you have read, the early 1920s were good economic times for Florida. These good times didn't last forever, though. By 1925 Florida's economy was starting to suffer. Eventually, Florida experienced a land **bust**. A bust refers to financial ruin. Read on to learn about the bust.

1925

As you know, the price of land had been driven up during the land boom. During the boom, people were buying land quickly in the hope of making a profit later by selling it. Sometimes they didn't bother to go look at the land they were buying. Some dishonest people, hoping to make lots of money, sold poor quality land—including land that was under water! This dishonesty and the high prices of land all helped turn the land boom into a land bust.

The winter of 1925 was extremely cold for Florida, and the summer afterward was very hot. This swing in the weather scared tourists and land buyers away, contributing to the land bust.

 In the chart below, write the causes and effects of Florida's land bust. One cause has been filled in for you.

Cause	Effect
cold winter and hot summer	

1926

In 1926 a hurricane hit Miami, destroying much of the city and its resort hotels. Only two years later, another hurricane caused Lake Okeechobee to overflow and flood many nearby towns. More than 2,000 people died. The damage caused by these hurricanes hurt tourism and added to the land bust. Florida's economy slowed even more.

1929

In 1929 a pest called the Mediterranean fruit fly killed most of Florida's citrus crops. To stop the fly from hurting crops in other parts of the country, the U.S. government decided not to allow Florida to sell any fruit that survived. As a result, Florida's farmers weren't able to make their usual money from citrus fruits.

The end of the land boom, the two hurricanes, and the damage to the citrus crop all led to an economic **depression** in Florida. A depression is a period of severe economic hardship. While Florida was already experiencing hard times, national events would only make the suffering worse. In October 1929, the national stock market crashed, sending the whole country into the deepest economic trouble it had ever seen.

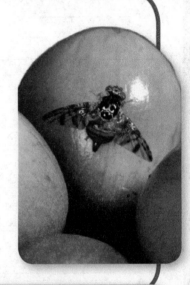

(t) Courtesy of the State Archives of Florida, (b) Photo by Scott Bauer/USDA

NGSS Standards
SS.4.A.7.1 Describe the causes and effects of the 1920's Florida land boom and bust.

Lesson 3

(?) Essential Question   Why do societies change?

_____

_____

_____

_____

Go back to _Show As You Go!_ on pages 124–125.

networks
connected.mcgraw-hill.com
● Games ● Assessment

© Corbis

Lesson 4 Florida and the Great Depression

? Essential Question

Why do societies change?
What do you think?

_____

_____

_____

_____

_____

_____

_____

Words To Know

Look at the words below. Tell a partner what you already know about these words.

Great Depression

stock

*approximately

relief

New Deal

Imagine going to the bank to take out money that you've been saving up. Wouldn't you be surprised if the bank told you that your money was gone? What would you do?

_____

_____

At the start of the **Great Depression** in 1929, many people in Florida and the United States found themselves in the situation described above. The Great Depression lasted through the 1930s. During this time, many people were very poor, and many did not have jobs.

There were many causes of the Great Depression. One cause had to do with the stock market. In the 1920s, a lot of people got rich by buying and selling **stocks**. Stocks are shares in the ownership of a company. Unfortunately, many people didn't buy and sell stocks responsibly. They borrowed money to buy stocks, which means they used money they didn't have.

What do you think is happening in this photo?

_____

_____

_____

150

The Crash

In October 1929, stock prices fell sharply and suddenly. Some people panicked, sold their stock, and stopped buying goods. This made stock prices fall even more. Prices fell so much that the stock market "crashed." Many stocks became worthless. People who had borrowed money to buy stocks could not repay their debts and they became financially ruined. Banks, having invested much of their money in stocks, were ruined too. These banks had been using people's money to invest in stocks. Therefore, when these banks closed, people lost any money that they had been saving there. Over the course of the Great Depression, over 5,000 banks nationwide closed due to failure.

(t) © Corbis, (b) Courtesy of the State Archives of Florida

▲ Some people lost everything in the stock market crash.

NGSS Standards
SS.4.A.1.1 Analyze primary and secondary sources to identify significant individuals and events throughout Florida history. **SS.4.A.6.3** Describe the contributions of significant individuals to Florida **SS.4.A.7.2** Summarize challenges Floridians faced during the Great Depression.

Reading Skill

Integrate Information

Reread pages 150–151. Then read the quote below. Write what you learned about the Great Depression from both sources.

In 1933, Florida author Marjorie Kinnan Rawlings wrote to her editor about the Depression. You'll learn more about her later.

"Do things look any brighter financially in New York? A Tampa friend . . . got us word . . . to get our [money] out of our Ocala bank in a hurry—the inside word is that 26 Florida banks are folding on Monday. . . . The world infection is beginning to spread. . . ."

▲ Marjorie Kinnan Rawlings

_____

_____

_____

Many families who lost their homes moved into "Hoovervilles." ▶

NGSS Standards
SS.4.A.7.2 Summarize challenges Floridians faced during the Great Depression.

▲ During the Depression, people lined up for meals at soup kitchens.

Challenges for Florida

As you have already learned, Florida was struggling economically even before the stock market crash. After the crash, more banks and businesses closed. When businesses closed, people lost their jobs. By 1933 **approximately** one in four workers did not have a job.

Without jobs, people couldn't afford their homes, and many lost them. People moved into tent cities that sprang up in Florida and across the country. These tent cities were called "Hoovervilles." They were named after Herbert Hoover, who was President in 1929. Many Americans blamed him for not stopping the Depression.

With little money, Floridians also had trouble paying for food, clothing, medical care, and other needs. Times were very tough, and people started to look to the government for help.

Eventually, Hoover started some programs to provide **relief**. Relief is help sometimes given in the form of financial aid. One of these programs gave relief money to banks and other businesses. These businesses were then supposed to help local people. Many Floridians were helped by these relief programs. But for a lot of people, these programs weren't enough.

Imagine that you are living through the Great Depression in Florida. Summarize the challenges that you face every day.

_____

_____

_____

_____

(t) Getty Images/Hulton Archive,(b) e Corbis

The New Deal

Upset with Hoover, Americans elected a new President in 1933. President Franklin Delano Roosevelt had a plan to help the country recover from the Great Depression. Roosevelt started a series of programs called the **New Deal**. The New Deal put people to work throughout the country.

One New Deal program was called the Civilian Conservation Corps (CCC). About 40,000 Floridians joined the CCC. They planted around 13 million trees in Florida and created many state parks and wildlife preserves. Other workers built federal buildings and schools.

One of the largest projects of the CCC was the Overseas Highway. This highway connected Miami and Key West. It helped the economic recovery of Key West by boosting tourism.

Another New Deal program was the Works Progress Administration (WPA). It employed about 40,000 Floridians on many different building projects. The WPA also provided jobs for researchers, writers, and editors.

Build for your NAVY!

ENLIST!
CARPENTERS, MACHINISTS, ELECTRICIANS ETC.
FOR INFORMATION APPLY TO YOUR NEAREST RECRUITING STATION
U.S. NAVY - BUREAU OF YARDS & DOCKS

▲ Projects like the WPA also encouraged people to enlist in the military.

President Franklin D. Roosevelt ▼

Marjorie Kinnan Rawlings

Even in the middle of economic hardship, Florida authors continued to write. Marjorie Kinnan Rawlings was one such author. She moved to Florida in 1928, and over the next 14 years, she wrote five novels. Her most famous, *The Yearling*, was published in 1938. It was at the top of the best-seller list for almost two years, which is impressive since people had little money to spend during the Depression. One reason for her success was that people identified with her characters. These characters were often poor and experiencing hard times, just like the people reading them.

▲ **Alfred Dupont**

Economic Recovery

The New Deal didn't fix the economy all at once. It took awhile for the economy to recover. A wealthy businessman, Alfred Dupont, helped too. He bought a few Florida banks and helped them start back up again. He also bought acres of forestland. He used this land to build up the paper industry in Florida. After Dupont died in 1935, his brother-in-law, Ed Ball, took over the paper mill business, adding to what Dupont had intended to do. These paper mills employed thousands of Floridians, helping the struggling economy. Ball was also in charge of the Florida National Bank. This bank had many branches in the state and was one of the strongest bank systems in Florida.

Slowly, Florida's other industries started to rebound. The citrus industry recovered from the fruit fly disaster. Farmers began to ship fruit all over the country again. Tourism started to come back, too, as people started to have some money to spend on travel. With more job opportunities and working banks, Florida started to come out of the Depression.

NGSS Standards
SS.4.A.6.3 Describe the contributions of significant individuals to Florida. **SS.4.E.1.1** Identify entrepreneurs from various social and ethnic backgrounds who have influenced Florida and local economy.

<u>Underline</u> the contributions that Marjorie Kinnan Rawlings made to Florida.

Match It Up!

 Match the people below with their contributions.

Marjorie Kinnan Rawlings •   • President who was blamed for the Great Depression

Ed Ball •   • helped Florida banks recover and started paper mill businesses

Franklin Delano Roosevelt •   • wrote books about rural Floridians and their lives

Alfred Dupont •   • in charge of large banking system in Florida

Herbert Hoover •   • President who started New Deal programs

 Topical Press Agency/Getty Images

Lesson 4

 Essential Question   Why do societies change?

_____

_____

_____

_____

_____

Go back to *Show As You Go!* on pages 124–125. ≪

 **networks**

connected.mcgraw-hill.com
• Games • Assessments

Florida in World War II

? Essential Question

How does conflict affect people?
What do you think?

_____

_____

_____

_____

_____

_____

_____

Have you ever worked with a group of people to meet a goal? If you have, you know that everyone had to do their part to help out. In this lesson, you'll learn about how Floridians worked together to help the United States during a crisis.

Florida and the rest of the United States suffered much during the Great Depression. During the 1930s, countries around the world were hurting too. In Germany, a man named Adolf Hitler took advantage of this situation. He told Germans that he had a plan to fix their problems. Hitler became **dictator** of Germany in 1933. A dictator is a person who rules a country with total authority.

Part of Hitler's plan was to take over Europe. In 1939 Hitler invaded Poland, starting World War II. Italy joined Germany, and together they formed the Axis Powers. Japan later joined the Axis Powers as well. These countries fought against the Allied Powers of Great Britain, France, and the Soviet Union.

At first, the United States stayed out of the war. Then, in 1941, Japan attacked Pearl Harbor, Hawaii. Congress declared war, and the United States joined the side of the Allies.

Words To Know

Look at the words below. (Circle) the words you already know. Put a question mark next to the words that you don't know.

dictator

*setting

enlist

NGSS Standards
SS.4.G.1.4 Interpret political and physical maps using map elements (title, compass rose, cardinal directions, intermediate directions, symbols, legend, scale, longitude, latitude).

Europe

Map and Globe Skills

Use the map key to color Italy, France, Germany, and the Soviet Union to show if they were Allied Powers or Axis Powers.

Florida Helps the War Effort

Once the United States entered the war, the whole country started to mobilize. Florida helped the war effort in several ways. Florida's long coastline made it ideal as a **setting** to build naval bases and shipyards. More than 100 warships were built in Florida during the war. Florida's flat land was perfect for airplanes too. Airplanes need lots of open, flat space to take off and land. By the mid 1940s, up to 40 airfields in Florida had new pilots training on them.

Across the country, people **enlisted** in the armed forces. To enlist means to volunteer for military service. Over 250,000 soldiers came from Florida. These soldiers needed training. Florida's warm climate and acres of empty land were ideal for military training. Just like naval bases and airfields, army bases were built all over the state. One of them, Camp Blanding, became Florida's fourth-largest city during the war. From 1940 to 1945, over 800,000 soldiers received training there. In all, Florida had 172 military bases during the war.

The military also needed food to feed its soldiers. Florida helped here too. Its year-round growing season made it the ideal place to grow food for the troops.

▲ Soldiers train on the beaches of Florida

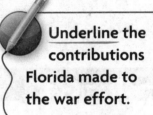
Underline the contributions Florida made to the war effort.

NGSS Standards
SS.4.A.7.3 Identify Florida's role in World War II.

Camp Blanding ▼

Action Close to Home

Most of the fighting in World War II happened in Europe. But did you know that some fighting took place just off the coast of Florida? Ten weeks after the Pearl Harbor attack, a German submarine entered Florida's waters and sank an American ship. From January to August of 1942, German submarines, or U-Boats, attacked more than 24 American ships off Florida's coast. Some of these happened so close to shore that tourists could see what was happening from their hotel balconies.

During the summer of 1942, one of these submarines slipped into the peaceful waters near Jacksonville at Ponte Vedra. It let four German spies ashore. Their mission was to blow up a railroad depot to stop the flow of supplies going to Allied troops. Luckily, officials caught the spies before they could go through with their plan.

These captured spies and other German prisoners of war (POWs) were sometimes held in Florida. Some POW camps were in military bases, where prisoners were put to work. These prisoners even had to help the Allied war effort by harvesting crops. Others were put to work cleaning city streets.

Reading Skill

Draw Inferences

Why do you think Germany attacked the United States in Florida?

_____

_____

_____

_____

Hotels Come in Handy

The many hotels in Florida also helped with the war effort. As you've already learned, the government planned to use Florida for military bases. But building bases takes a lot of time. The government wanted to train soldiers as quickly as possible. So instead of constructing new buildings, the government decided to use hotels. Florida already had a lot of hotels because of the popular tourist business all over the state. Using hotels for the military meant that the government wouldn't have to spend time or money to build new buildings. These hotels became military housing, schools for soldiers, hospitals, and recovery centers for soldiers who were injured during training. Throughout the war, the federal government used over 500 resort hotels in Florida. By itself, the air force, one of the branches of the military, used 70,000 hotel rooms in Miami Beach. By late 1943, though, all these hotels were empty as soldiers shipped overseas to Europe.

Underline how Florida contributed to the war effort

U-Boat Attacks in Florida Waters, 1942

Map and Globe Skills

1. Find the farthest U-Boat attack from Florida using the map scale. How far is it from the coast?

_____

2. Why do you think many U-Boat attacks happened on Florida's east coast?

_____

_____

NGSS Standards
SS.4.A.7.3 Identify Florida's role in World War II.
SS.4.G.1.4 Interpret political and physical maps using map elements (title, compass rose, cardinal directions, intermediate directions, symbols, legend, scale, longitude, latitude).

Citizens Help

Everyday people did their part to aid the war effort. Read the memory book page below to learn how ordinary Floridians made a difference.

Andrew's Memory Book

Even kids are helping the war effort with scrap drives.

Journal - May 13, 1942

Everyone in Florida is helping the war effort in any way they can. In town, I've seen them helping by donating to scrap drives. In a scrap drive, the government collects any pieces of metal, such as pots and pans, that people can spare. This metal will then be melted down and reused to make tanks or airplanes. People are also planting gardens to produce food for the war effort. Any area of land is a possible garden—backyards, schoolyards, city parks, and empty lots. The government is encouraging people to grow these "victory gardens" with posters and announcements on the radio. Just the other day, city officials in Tampa announced that the city had over 10,000 victory gardens.

WAR ENDS! *August 14, 1945*

Breaking news! The Allies have won the war! Germany is defeated, Japan has surrendered, and the world is celebrating!

We expect Florida servicemen and women to return home soon. Tens of thousands of the soldiers who trained here also plan to return to Florida. Many of them will most likely bring their families too. Maybe they'll stay here permanently! Florida's population is expected to increase.

Soldiers celebrate the end of the war.

Read the letter below and fill in the blanks with words from the box on the right.

Camp Blanding
U-Boats
victory
Florida
Europe
weather

Dear Mother,

How are you? I guess you and Dad will be getting ready for the harvest. I wish I could see how much food you've grown in your

_____ garden.

Training goes well at _____. The food isn't bad, and I'm making lots of friends in my squad.

Don't believe everything you read in the newspapers. Sure, there are

some _____ here and there, but they can't hurt folks on shore. Subs only attack ships. The navy is working on a plan to stop them.

Yesterday, we went to the beach for training. We all hope to leave

soon for _____.

Earlier today, a whole group of fighter planes flew overhead! We're

seeing them more as the airfields all over _____ get

trainees. We're very lucky to have such nice _____ in Florida. It makes training easier and faster.

Take care of yourself and try not to worry about me.

Your son,
Andrew

Lesson 5

 Essential Question How does conflict affect people?

_____

_____

_____

Go back to *Show As You Go!* on pages 124–125.

 netw⊙rks

connected.mcgraw-hill.com
● Games ● Assessment

161

Florida and the Civil Rights Movement

Essential Question

Why are civil rights important?
What do you think?

_____

_____

_____

_____

Words To Know

Draw the symbol next to each word to show how much you know about its meaning.

? = I have no idea!
▲ = I know a little.
★ = I know a lot.

civil rights

integration

discrimination

civil disobedience

boycott

*alter

How do you get to school? Do you walk, take a bus, or get dropped off by car? How long does it take you to get to school each day?

_____

_____

_____

Long ago, most children walked to school every day. Mary McLeod Bethune was a young African American girl who had to walk several miles to school and back each day. She didn't mind, though, because she knew that getting a good education was very important.

When Bethune was alive, African Americans were not allowed to go to the same schools as whites because of segregation. Remember that segregation is the separation of people based on race. At this time, most African American schools weren't as good as schools for whites. Bethune thought that everyone deserved a good education, so she started her own school for African American girls in 1904. The school was located in Daytona Beach.

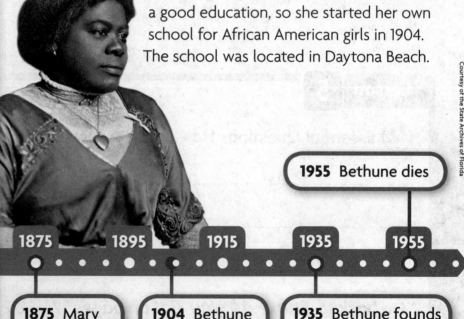

1955 Bethune dies

| 1875 | 1895 | 1915 | 1935 | 1955 |

1875 Mary McLeod Bethune is born

1904 Bethune opens school in Daytona Beach, Florida

1935 Bethune founds the National Council of Negro Women

Working for Civil Rights

NGSS Standards
SS.4.A.6.3 Describe the contributions of significant individuals to Florida.

Bethune was an early leader in the **civil rights** movement. Civil rights are the rights of every citizen to be treated equally under the law. The civil rights movement worked to gain African Americans the same rights as white people in our country.

In addition to her school, Bethune helped the civil rights movement in another way. In 1935 she founded the National Council of Negro Women, an organization dedicated to helping African American women and their families.

Years after Mary McLeod Bethune started her school, other people continued to work for civil rights for African Americans. For example, during World War II, the National Association for the Advancement of Colored People (NAACP) worked for African American civil rights throughout the South, including Florida. The organization hoped to end segregation. They wanted **integration**. Integration is the act of bringing the races together and making something open to all people. It is the opposite of segregation.

DID YOU KNOW?
Bethune's school still exists today! It is now called Bethune-Cookman University and accepts both male and female students.

Underline the contributions Bethune made to Florida.

Bettmann/CORBIS

◀ Mary McLeod Bethune and other civil rights leaders visit President Harry Truman at the White House.

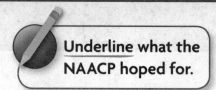

Underline what the NAACP hoped for.

Fighting Segregation

By fighting segregation, the NAACP was also fighting **discrimination**. Discrimination is an unfair difference in the way people are treated. For example, discrimination kept African Americans from getting jobs because some employers refused to hire them because of their race.

The NAACP started what was called the "Double V" campaign during World War II. The two "Vs" stood for victory against dictators overseas and victory against racism at home. They wanted to defeat Hitler in Europe and racism in the United States. The Florida NAACP wanted to bring attention to segregation in hopes of ending it. They published articles, photos, and drawings in newspapers to promote the campaign.

One man who helped the NAACP's cause was Floridian James Weldon Johnson. Johnson was a teacher and a writer. He wrote many poems, books, and songs that described the lives of African Americans in the early 1900s. His song, "Lift Ev'ry Voice and Sing," eventually became the official song of the NAACP.

▲ James Weldon Johnson

NGSS Standards
SS.4.A.6.3 Describe the contributions of significant individuals to Florida. **SS.4.A.8.1** Identify Florida's role in the Civil Rights Movement.

People in Florida marching to our state capitol in Tallahassee in a peaceful demonstration to support the civil rights movement. ▼

Describe the contribution that James Weldon Johnson made.

_____

_____

NAACP lawyer Thurgood Marshall helped fight segregation too. Almost 60 years earlier, the Supreme Court had said that "separate but equal," or segregated, places were constitutional. Marshall wanted to show that segregated places were not really equal. In 1954 he argued in the case *Brown* v. *the Board of Education of Topeka, Kansas*, that African American children were being poorly educated in segregated schools. The Supreme Court ruled in Marshall's favor, saying that segregation in public schools was unconstitutional.

The NAACP also encouraged **civil disobedience**. Civil disobedience is refusing to follow laws considered unfair in order to bring change. For example, a law common in the South said that African Americans had to give up their seats to white people on buses when the buses were full. One day in December 1955, an African American woman named Rosa Parks decided not to follow this unfair law. When she refused to give up her bus seat to a white person, she was arrested and jailed. Her actions sparked major changes in the fight for civil rights, not only in Alabama, but throughout the South, including Florida.

▲ **Students had to attend segregated schools.**

▲ Students protest city bus segregation.

(t) © Bettmann/CORBIS. (b) Courtesy of the State Archives of Florida

NGSS Standards
SS.4.A.8.1 Identify Florida's role in the Civil Rights Movement.

▲ Dr. Martin Luther King, Jr., speaks in St. Augustine

Protests Continue

In Montgomery, to protest Rosa Parks's arrest, African Americans started a **boycott** of the bus system. To boycott is to refuse to do business with a person, group, company, or country. The boycott worked, and the unfair bus law in Alabama was changed.

African Americans in Florida also faced discrimination on buses. Following Rosa Parks's example, in 1956 two African American women in Tallahassee also refused to give up their bus seats to white people. Like Parks, they were arrested. To protest, the African American community in Tallahassee began their own bus boycott. Before long, Tallahassee officials **altered** the law. African Americans could then sit wherever they wanted on the bus.

Another protest method that people who worked for civil rights used was sit-ins. African American students staged these sit-ins at lunch counters of restaurants that were labeled for "whites only." They sat down and refused to leave until they were served. One of these sit-ins happened in Florida in 1959. Over time, sit-ins led to many restaurants being integrated.

Reading Skill

Draw Inferences

How does a boycott affect businesses?

_____

_____

_____

In 1963 Dr. Martin Luther King, Jr., a leader in the civil rights movement, and other leaders organized a march on Washington, D.C. In August of that year, 250,000 people gathered in the city. The march ended with King's powerful "I Have a Dream" speech. The march on Washington led to the passage of the Civil Rights Act of 1964. The Civil Rights Act prohibited discrimination in public places, education, work places, and voter registration. It also banned discrimination based on race, religion, and gender.

In 1964 Dr. Martin Luther King, Jr., traveled to St. Augustine. He encouraged people there to change society through nonviolent methods. He told the people in the crowd to be respectful to one another. While in St. Augustine, he organized a march to support integration. Unfortunately, violence broke out between marchers and people who supported segregation.

▲ Segregation happened everywhere, even on public beaches.

Leaders Help

Florida Governor LeRoy Collins was in office from 1955 to 1961. During this time, he helped Florida's process of integration. He set up a statewide multi-racial committee and appointed several African American community leaders to it. He hoped that the committee would help Florida integrate gradually and peacefully. Also, in 1960, he encouraged integration in a speech. Because of this slow but steady progress, the violence around integration that happened in other Southern states didn't happen as much in Florida. After he left office, Collins helped get the national Civil Rights Act of 1964 passed.

▲ Governor LeRoy Collins

Underline the way Governor Collins helped Florida integrate.

NGSS Standards
SS.4.A.8.1 Identify Florida's role in the Civil Rights Movement.

Civil Rights for Others

Since the 1960s, other groups have sought equal rights too. Protests were organized for improved working conditions, equal pay, and fair treatment.

In 1962 Mexican Americans organized a group to help migrant farm workers. Migrant farm workers travel around from farm to farm to plant and harvest crops. This group brought higher wages and better working conditions to migrant workers.

In 1966 women organized to gain equal pay. The National Organization for Women (NOW) forced the government to enforce the Civil Rights Act of 1964, which made it against the law to discriminate against women in the workplace.

In 1990 the Americans with Disabilities Act (ADA) made it illegal to discriminate against people with disabilities. It also required all public facilities to be accessible to people with disabilities.

▲ President Lyndon B. Johnson signs the Civil Rights Act of 1964 into law.

Reading Skill

Interpret Information

What does the chart tell you about the progress of civil rights?

_____

_____

_____

_____

_____

_____

Date	What Happened	Why This Is Important
1962	César Chávez and Dolores Huerta found the National Farm Workers Association (NFWA).	The NFWA led strikes and boycotts to bring better wages and working conditions to migrant farm workers. Many of these workers were Hispanic.
1966	The National Organization for Women (NOW) is founded.	NOW fought for equal opportunities for women, such as equal pay for equal work.
1990	The Americans with Disabilities Act (ADA) becomes law.	ADA made it illegal to discriminate against people with disabilities.

Look at the time line. On the lines for each date, write the event or events that happened that year. Then follow the directions in the box.

Draw a picture for the event that happened in Florida in 1956.

NGSS Standards
SS.4.A.8.1 Identify Florida's role in the Civil Rights Movement. **SS.4.A.9.1** Utilize timelines to sequence key events in Florida history.

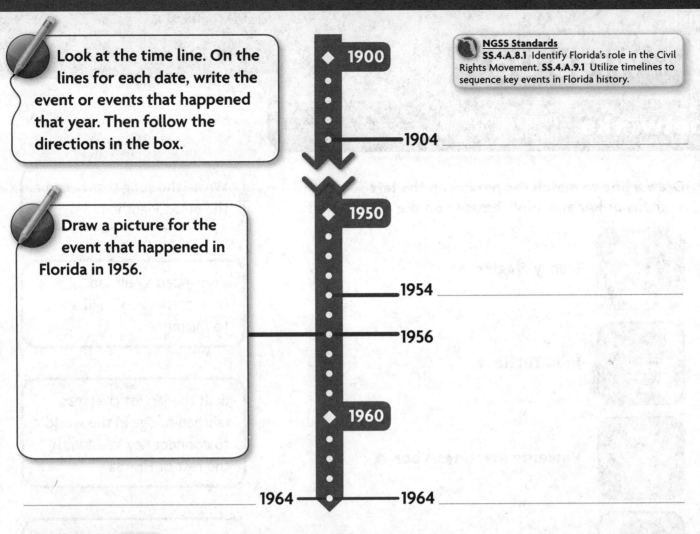

◆ 1900

———— 1904 _____

◆ 1950

———— 1954 _____

———— 1956

◆ 1960

1964 ————— 1964 _____

Lesson 6

? **Essential Question** Why are civil rights important?

_____

_____

_____

_____

_____

_____

Go back to *Show As You Go!* on pages 124–125.

Draw a line to match the person on the left with his or her accomplishments on the right.

 Henry Flagler ●

 Julia Tuttle ●

 Vincente Martínez Ybor ●

 John Gorrie ●

 Thomas Alva Edison ●

 Marjorie Kinnan Rawlings ●

 **James Weldon Johnson** ●

 Mary McLeod Bethune ●

● Wrote the song that became the NAACP anthem

● Convinced a railroad entrepreneur to build a line to Miami

● Built the largest overseas railroad bridge in the world to connect Key West with the rest of Florida

● Founded a school for African American girls

● Invented the basic concept for air conditioning

● Raised money for the Cuban independence movement, owned a cigar factory

● Helped invent the light bulb and many other machines

● Wrote the young adult classic *The Yearling*

Unit Project

Imagine that you are a reporter for a Florida newspaper. Choose one event from this unit, and write an article about it as if you were there. Why did this event happen? What happened as a result of this event? Before you begin, look back at **Show As You Go!** on pages 124–125 to review your notes. Read the list below to see what should be included in your article. As you work, check off each task.

> **Florida's Economy Bust!**
>
> "The good days are behind us," said a local from St Augustine as Florida's economic hardships worsened. Things might have recovered after the land boom and bust, but with two hurricanes hitting our state within 3 years, recovery looks very far away.

NGSS Standards
SS.4.A.1.2 Synthesize information related to Florida history through print and electronic media.

Your newspaper article should...	Yes, it does!
describe who was involved in the event.	☐
tell where and when the event happened.	☐
explain why the event took place and what happened during it.	☐
explain the causes and effects of the event.	☐
include at least one image of the event.	☐
include information from at least two electronic or print media sources.	☐
use correct spelling, grammar, and punctuation.	☐

Think about the Big Idea

BIG IDEA Change happens over time.

What did you learn in this unit that helps you understand the BIG IDEA?

_____

_____

_____

Read the passage "Marjorie Kinnan Rawlings" and then answer Numbers 1 and 2.

Marjorie Kinnan Rawlings

1   MARJORIE Kinnan Rawlings always loved to write, even as a little girl. When she was only 11 years old, she had one of her stories published in a large newspaper. She also won a writing contest when she was 11. But it wasn't until she moved to Florida in 1928 that she really began to find her voice as a writer.

2   She moved to Cross Creek, near Gainesville, where she decided to grow oranges and pursue her writing. The rural setting of Cross Creek gave her so much inspiration that within the next several years she wrote five books. Her first book was called *South Moon Under*.

3   Rawlings's most famous book is called *The Yearling*. It's about a young boy in rural Florida who adopts an orphaned fawn. It was so popular when it was published in 1938 that it was eventually made into a movie in 1946. You can still read this book today! She also published *Golden Apples, Cross Creek*, and a cookbook. You can visit her house and farm which are now National Historic Landmarks.

"Marjorie Kinnan Rawlings" property of McGraw-Hill Education.

GO ON →

Now answer Numbers 1 and 2. Base your answers on the passage "Marjorie Kinnan Rawlings."

1 Read this sentence from paragraph 2.

"The rural setting of Cross Creek gave her so much inspiration that within the next several years she wrote five books."

What does <u>inspiration</u> mean as it is used in this sentence?

(A) a kind of sickness

(B) a feeling of creativity

(C) a large sum of money

(D) a kind of dance

2 This question has two parts. First, answer Part A. Then, answer Part B.

Part A What is the main idea of this passage?

(A) Rawlings liked to write as a young girl.

(B) Rawlings was a terrible writer.

(C) Rawlings wrote many stories throughout her life.

(D) Rawlings knew everything about writing.

Part B Which sentence from the passage supports the answer in Part A?

(A) "Marjorie Kinnan Rawlings always loved to write, even as a little girl."

(B) "When she was only 11 years old, she had one of her stories published in a large newspaper."

(C) "She also won a writing contest when she was 11."

(D) "But it wasn't until she moved to Florida in 1928 that she really began to find her voice as a writer."

GO ONLINE to connected.mcgraw-hill.com for enhanced Florida Test Preparation options, available through Engrade.

Florida's People, Economy, and Government

BIG IDEA

Culture influences the way people live.

Florida is a state of many different cultures. Americans from cold winter climates, especially retired people, often move to Florida. In fact, the state has the highest percentage of people over 65 in the country. Florida also has a large Jewish community. Florida is home to many immigrants too. In this unit, you will read about how and why immigrants impact our state. You will also read about our state's economy and government. Did you know that Florida has the fourth largest state economy in the United States? Businesses and people are attracted to the many opportunities Florida offers them. As you read this unit, think about how our people, economy, and government influence the way we live.

netw⊙rks

connected.mcgraw-hill.com
◉ Skill Builders
◉ Vocabulary Flashcards

Show As You Go!

After you read each lesson in this unit, choose a public issue in Florida that is related to the topic of the lesson. Describe the issue below. You will use your notes here to help you complete a project at the end of this unit.

Fold page here.

Lesson 1

_____
_____
_____
_____

Lesson 2

_____
_____
_____
_____

Lesson 3

_____
_____
_____
_____
_____

Lesson 4

_____
_____
_____
_____

NGSS Standards
LAFS.4.RI.3.8 Explain how an author uses reasons and evidence to support particular points in a text.

Explain Author's Purpose

When authors write, they make points that they share with readers. Authors might try to be convincing or informative. They might also want to explain the causes and effects of an event. Authors support their points with reasons and evidence. Using reasons and evidence makes an author's writing strong. Recognizing the points authors make and the reasons and evidence they use to support these points will help you understand what you read.

LEARN IT

- **Figure out the point that the author is making. An author's point is also usually the main idea of a passage. Authors sometimes make more than one point in a passage.**

- **Then look for reasons and evidence that support the author's point(s). Reasons and evidence are details in the passage.**

Did you know that many people don't vote in elections? Voting is so important! Everyone should vote! Our government needs citizens to be involved in it in order for it to work. Voting is a great way to take part in our government. Our government also needs good leaders, lawmakers, and judges. Citizens need to choose these people in elections. People should have a say in things that affect their lives. When they vote, citizens give their opinions about how their communities should be run.

Author's reason

Author's point

Momentum Creative Group / Alamy

◀ **People vote for their elected officials.**

TRY IT

Fill in the chart below with the author's point from the paragraph on page 176. Then fill in the reasons and evidence the author uses to support his points.

Author's Point

Reasons and Evidence

APPLY IT

- Review the steps for explaining an author's purpose in Learn It.
- Read the passage below. Underline the author's point. Then circle reasons and evidence the author uses to support her point.

Walt Disney World has something for everyone! People of all ages will find many things they enjoy at the resort's four theme parks. Visitors can ride fun rides, see interesting exhibits, and get their pictures taken with loveable characters. The resort also has plenty of things to eat and many shopping options. Walt Disney World Resort has something to interest everyone. They have exhibits that will teach you about U.S. Presidents, cars, other countries, movie making, animals, technology, and everything in between.

Words to Know

NGSS Standards
LAFS.4.RI.2.4 Determine the meaning of general academic and domain-specific words or phrases in a text relevant to a grade 4 topic or subject area.

The list below shows some important words you will learn in this unit. Their definitions can be found on the next page. Read the words.

heritage (HEHR • uh • tihj) (p. 184)

ethnic group (ETH • nihk GROOP) (p. 185)

interdependent (ihn• tuhr • dih • PEHN • duhnt) (p. 194)

export (eks • PORT) (p. 194)

legislative branch (LEHJ • uh • slay • tihv BRANCH) (p. 197)

recycle (ree • SY • kuhl) (p. 200)

petition (puh • TIH • shuhn) (p. 201)

conservation (kahn • suhr • VAY • shuhn) (p. 201)

FOLDABLES

The Foldable on the next page will help you learn these important words. Follow the steps below to make your Foldable.

Step 1 Fold along the solid red line.

Step 2 Cut along the dotted lines.

Step 3 Read the words and their definitions.

Step 4 Complete the activities on each tab.

Step 5 Look at the back of your Foldable. Choose ONE of these activities for each word to help you remember its meaning:

- Draw a picture of the word.

- Write a description of the word.

- Write how the word is related to something you know.

Heritage is the way of life that has been handed down from the past.

Write an example of your heritage.

An **ethnic group** is a group of people from the same country or with a shared culture.

Write two examples of ethnic groups.

_____ _____

Countries that rely on each other to meet the needs and wants of their people are **interdependent**.

Write the root word of *interdependent*.

An **export** is something that is sold or traded to another country.

Write the antonym, or opposite, of *export*.

The **legislative branch** of government makes laws.

Write an example of a law.

To **recycle** is to make something new from something that has been used before.

Write two examples of things people recycle.

_____ _____

A **petition** is a formal request made to a person of authority.

What would you petition the government for?

Conservation is the protection and careful use of natural resources.

What is the root word of *conservation*?

heritage

heritage

CUT HERE

ethnic group

ethnic group

interdependent

interdependent

export

export

legislative branch

legislative branch

recycle

recycle

petition

petition

conservation

conservation

Primary Sources

NGSS Standards
SS.4.A.1.1 Analyze primary and secondary sources to identify significant individuals and events throughout Florida history.
SS.4.A.1.2 Synthesize information related to Florida history through print and electronic media.

Photographs

Photographs capture events as they happen and show what people and places looked like at a specific time. Newspapers and Web sites are two places where you can often see photographs. To analyze a photograph, ask yourself questions about it. When was it taken? What are the people in the photo doing? How do they look? What action is taking place in the photo? What objects are shown in the photograph? The answers to these questions will help you understand what life was like when the photo was taken.

 Document-Based Questions

**Examine the two photographs on this page.
Use them to answer the questions below.**

1. **Describe what is happening in the top photograph.**

   _____

2. **Describe what is happening in the bottom photograph.**

   _____

3. **Synthesize, or combine, your information about these photos. What do both of these photographs tell you about workers?**

   _____

   _____

(t) Gary John Norman / Getty Images, (b) NASA Kennedy Space Center (NASA-KSC)

networks
There's More Online!
● Skill Builders
● Resource Library

Impact of Immigration

How does immigration affect a place?
What do you think?

_____

_____

_____

_____

_____

_____

Florida is a state of many immigrants. Why do you think immigrants come to Florida? Write your thoughts below.

_____

_____

_____

_____

Immigrants have been coming to Florida for hundreds of years. They come here for many reasons. Many come for job opportunities or to live in safety and freedom. Others come for our bright sunshine and mild weather. No matter what the reason, immigrants make Florida a **unique** place with a culture all its own.

Immigrants becoming U.S. citizens. ▼

Morton Beebe/CORBIS

Words To Know

Look at the words below. Rank them 1 (know well) to 4 (know least) based on how much you know about them.

____ *unique

____ refugee

____ heritage

____ ethnic group

NGSS Standards
SS.4.A.8.2 Describe how and why immigration impacts Florida today.

Florida's Immigrants

Many immigrants come to Florida to escape conditions in their home countries. Sometimes immigrants' home countries become unsafe places to live. For example, in the 1970s, a group of people in Haiti were being killed for speaking out against the government. In 1972 the first **refugees** from Haiti started arriving in Florida. A refugee is a person who flees a place to find safety or protection somewhere else. Other refugees have come to Florida so that they can live in freedom in the United States.

Not everyone comes to Florida because of harsh conditions in their home countries. People from countries with cold winter climates, like Canada, come to Florida for our mild climate. Others come here because of our state's diverse people. Many of our state's immigrants come from Latin American countries, such as Cuba.

Many Cubans live in a neighborhood called Little Havana. It is a center of social, cultural, and political activity for Cubans living in Miami. Florida and Cuba have a long history of cultural influence dating back to the 1500s. Between 1959 and 1980, over 625,000 Cubans came to Florida because of disagreements with Cuba's communist government. Today, Little Havana has many of the cultural influences of Cuba, including food, language, and architecture.

> Underline the impact immigrants have on Florida.

DID YOU KNOW?
In 1980 the economy of Cuba took a dramatic downturn. Cuban Americans in Florida organized the Mariel Boatlift. This boatlift brought about 125,000 Cubans by boat from Cuba's Mariel Harbor to Florida. They became a part of Florida's Cuban community.

▼ Cuban refugees walk through a temporary refugee camp in Florida.

©Bettmann/Corbis

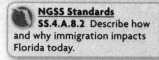
A Mix of Cultures

Many Floridians are either immigrants or are related to immigrants of the past. These people impact our state by sharing their cultures with others. They have shared their languages, festivals, and ways of life. Our **heritage**, or the way of life that has been handed down from the past, is reflected in the languages we speak and the holidays we celebrate.

Miami-Dade County

Immigrants live in all parts of Florida. However, the majority live in southern Florida. In fact, Miami-Dade is the only county in the entire country where more than half the people were not born in the United States. A mix of people from Cuba, Haiti, Columbia, Jamaica, Canada, Mexico, and Brazil make up most of the population of Miami-Dade County.

A Land of Many Languages

Over 200 languages are spoken in Florida. Although most people in Florida speak English, about 4 million of our 18.7 million people speak another language at home. Most of these people speak Spanish, a language that has been part of Florida's culture since the 1500s.

The second most common language spoken among immigrants in Florida is Haitian Creole. It is spoken by people from Haiti and is a mixture of French and African languages.

> **DID YOU KNOW?**
> Other languages widely spoken by immigrants in Florida include French, German, Portuguese, Italian, Tagalog (from the Philippines), Vietnamese, Arabic, and Russian.

Most Spoken Languages in Florida (other than English)

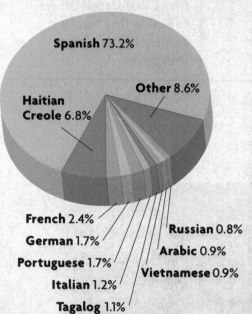

Spanish 73.2%
Other 8.6%
Haitian Creole 6.8%
French 2.4%
German 1.7%
Portuguese 1.7%
Italian 1.2%
Tagalog 1.1%
Russian 0.8%
Arabic 0.9%
Vietnamese 0.9%

▼ A mural in Little Haiti

JUAN CASTRO/AFP/Getty Images

Chart and Graph Skills

Use a Circle Graph

What is the most common non-English language spoken in Florida?

Calle Ocho

Many festivals that celebrate people's heritages take place all over Florida. The Calle Ocho (Eighth Street) festival in Little Havana is one of the largest street festivals in the world. Over a million visitors attend the annual festival. Different **ethnic groups**, or people from the same country or with a shared culture, wear colors or flags to show pride in their heritage. Many countries are celebrated during the Calle Ocho festival, including Cuba, Colombia, Venezuela, Nicaragua, the U.S. territory of Puerto Rico, the Dominican Republic, Costa Rica, and even Ireland. You can enjoy food from many different countries during the festival as you listen to music by many different ethnic groups.

(t) JUSTIN LANE/epa/CORBIS, (b) SEAN DRAKES/Alamy

◄ Gloria Estefan is a Cuban American singer involved in the Little Havana community.

▼ Calle Ocho in Little Havana

What ethnic food does your family enjoy?

_____

185

NGSS Standards
SS.4.A.8.2 Describe how and why immigration impacts Florida today. SS.4.A.1.1 Analyze primary and secondary resources to identify significant individuals and events throughout Florida history.

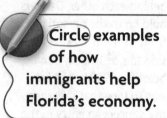

Circle examples of how immigrants help Florida's economy.

Economic Impact

Florida has a long history of immigrants contributing to our economic success. Since Florida became a state in 1845, immigrants have built roads, bridges, skyscrapers, and hospitals. They have worked as engineers, doctors, hotel and restaurant workers, and migrant farm workers. Without immigrants, Florida would not have the workers it needs to keep our economy strong. Even today, 23 percent of Florida workers are immigrants.

Because immigrants drive our economy, they contribute to Florida's ability to pay its bills. A study by the Florida International University found the state's immigrant workers pay an average of about $19 billion in taxes each year. This money helps pay for government services, such as schools and road construction.

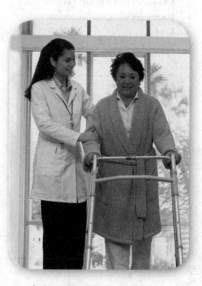

▲ Immigrants work in hospitals.

Immigrants work in construction. ▶

Reading Skill

Explain Author's Purpose

Read this excerpt from an article in *The Washington Post* by Governor Jeb Bush and professor of public policy Robert D. Putnam:

"Immigrants enhance [improve] our ability to grow and prosper in the dynamic global marketplace. We will need every possible advantage to expand our economy. . . . Moreover, the aging of our population places a premium on young, productive workers, many of whom must come from immigration."

List two reasons the authors give to support their view on immigration.

_____

_____

_____

_____

Immigrants' Impact on Florida

Fill in the chart to summarize how and why immigration impacts Florida today.

Social Impact	Economic Impact	Political Impact	Cultural Impact

(?) **Essential Question** How does immigration affect a place?

_____

_____

_____

_____

_____

_____

Go back to *Show As You Go!* on pages 174–175. ◀◀◀

There's More Online!
● Games ● Assessment

Florida's Economy

How does the economy affect people?
What do you think?

_____

_____

_____

_____

_____

_____

_____

If you had the opportunity to start a business, what kind of business would it be? Why would Florida be a good place for your business? Write your thoughts below.

_____

_____

_____

_____

Florida is home to many different kinds of businesses that help our state's economy grow. These companies are attracted to Florida for different reasons. One reason is our geography. Our state's long coastline and many ports attract businesses that trade with other countries. Our mild weather and climate also bring many companies to the state. Agricultural businesses are attracted to Florida because of our many natural resources. Finally, our **diverse** and skilled workforce has helped draw businesses to our state. All of these reasons have made Florida the fourth-largest state economy in the United States!

NASA Kennedy Space Center (NASA-KSC)

Words To Know

Look at the words below. Circle the words you already know. Put a question mark next to the words you don't know.

*diverse

*theme

interdependent

export

import

▼ The space shuttle is maintained by highly skilled workers.

Circle the reasons businesses are attracted to Florida.

NGSS Standards
SS.4.A.8.3 Describe the effect of the United States space program on Florida's economy and growth.

▲ The Rocket Garden at the Kennedy Space Center displays many historical rockets for tourists.

NASA Kennedy Space Center (NASA-KSC)

Florida's Space Industry

Florida's geography and weather have attracted one very important industry to our state—the space industry. In 1962 the National Aeronautics and Space Administration (NASA) decided to build Kennedy Space Center in Cape Canaveral. NASA chose Cape Canaveral because of its ocean front location. Launching space craft over an ocean is safer than launching it over land.

Kennedy Space Center created new job opportunities for Floridians. These jobs were at the space center itself and also at nearby companies that produced technology and equipment. These new high-tech companies developed and created the technology that rockets and spaceships required. The companies were located in towns and cities around Cape Canaveral. As a result, these towns and cities grew. Larger towns and cities needed more restaurants, schools, and shopping areas. All of this economic growth brought new people into our state. As a result, Florida's population grew.

How has the U.S. space program affected Florida's economy? Fill in the chart below.

Economic effects of the U.S. space program

189

Circle the natural resources of Florida on this page. Underline the fruits and vegetables grown here.

Agriculture

Industries that rely on Florida's natural resources also affect Florida's economy and growth. Florida's fertile soil and abundance of water allow for the growing of many kinds of plants. Citrus fruit, such as oranges, grapefruit, tangerines, lemons, and limes, are an important part of our state's economy. Today, Florida produces more than half of all the citrus fruit grown in the United States.

Florida farmers also produce many other crops. In fact, they produce more tomatoes, sugarcane, sweet corn, green beans, green peppers, watermelons, radishes, and eggplant than farmers in any other state.

Florida farmers are also a leading producer of plants that are for decoration only. Florida grows over 200 different types of plants, from small, delicate ferns to large palm trees.

John Coletti / Getty Images

▼ **An orange harvest**

Florida's Farm and Mineral Resources

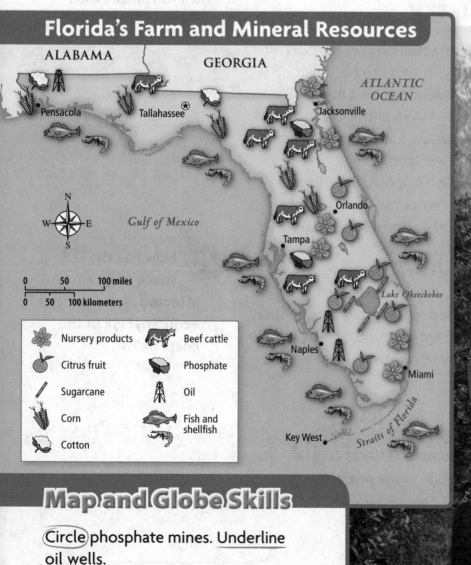

ALABAMA
GEORGIA
ATLANTIC OCEAN
Pensacola
Tallahassee
Jacksonville
Gulf of Mexico
Orlando
Tampa
Lake Okeechobee
Naples
Miami
Key West
Straits of Florida

N W E S

0   50   100 miles
0   50   100 kilometers

Legend:
- Nursery products
- Citrus fruit
- Sugarcane
- Corn
- Cotton
- Beef cattle
- Phosphate
- Oil
- Fish and shellfish

Map and Globe Skills

Circle phosphate mines. Underline oil wells.

Ranchers and Fishers

Did you know that Florida is also a major cattle-producing state? As you've read, people have been raising cattle in Florida since the first Spanish settlers arrived over 400 years ago. Today, Florida is one of the largest cattle-producing states east of the Mississippi River.

Most of our state's cattle ranches are found in southern Florida. Most young cattle are shipped out of our state while they are still young. Calves are shipped to other states, like Texas, where there is more open land for them to roam.

Many Florida farmers harvest their products from our state's water instead of from the soil. Many fishers work along our state's coastline to catch seafood. Florida fishers catch millions of pounds of fish, such as sea bass, flounder, grouper, and red snapper, each year. They also catch shellfish, such as shrimp, scallops, and oysters.

▲ Cattle and seafood are a large part of our state's economy.

Why is agriculture important to our state?

_____

_____

_____

NGSS Standards
SS.4.E.1.2 Explain Florida's role in the national and international economy and conditions that attract businesses to the state.

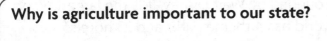

Phosphate

In unit 4 you read about the discovery of phosphate in Florida. Today, phosphate is still important to our economy. Bone Valley in central Florida produces 75 percent of the phosphate used in the United States. It also produces 25 percent of the world's supply of this mineral. The phosphate industry employs about 6,000 people directly and 30,000 indirectly. Exporting phosphate is the main reason that the port of Tampa is the 10th largest port in the United States.

Underline the number of people the phosphate industry employs indirectly.

NGSS Standards
SS.4.A.8.4 Explain how tourism affects Florida's economy and growth. **SS.4.G.1.4** Interpret political and physical maps using map elements (title, compass rose, cardinal directions, intermediate directions, symbols, legend, scale, longitude, latitude). **SS.4.E.1.1** Identify entrepreneurs from various social and ethnic backgrounds who have influenced Florida and local economy.

DID YOU KNOW?

Disney's success brought other theme parks, including Universal Orlando Resort, Busch Gardens, and SeaWorld to Florida. These parks have created many jobs in Florida. They have also made Florida one of the best places for people to vacation.

Underline how Walt Disney World affected our economy.

Tourism

As you read on page 189, the space industry has helped our economy grow. It has also helped another Florida industry—tourism. Kennedy Space Center is a major tourist attraction that brings about 1.5 million visitors to Florida each year. But visitors to our state enjoy many other attractions, including beach resorts, museums, sporting events, national parks, historic sites, and **theme** parks.

Tourism is very important to Florida. In fact, the tourism industry makes up the largest part of our state's economy! Year-round warm weather and our state's geography are two of the reasons that about 60 million visitors come to our state each year. Tourists spend money on attractions, at restaurants, on hotels, and in stores all across the state. These businesses provide thousands of jobs for Floridians.

Resorts and Theme Parks

The most popular stop for tourists in Florida is the Walt Disney World Resort near Orlando. Founded by Walt Disney, it is the largest resort in the world. Disney World has 4 theme parks and 23 hotels.

▼ Universal Studios in Orlando, Florida

John Greim/LightRocket/Getty Images

Natural Wonders

Florida also has many natural wonders. One of the most interesting parts of Florida is Everglades National Park. This park, which was founded in 1947, covers 1.5 million acres in southern Florida. That's larger than the entire state of Delaware! The Everglades is home to about 300 kinds of fish and 350 types of birds, including flamingos and egrets. There are also about 45 varieties of plants in the Everglades that grow nowhere else in the world.

Another of our national parks is mostly under water. Biscayne National Park is one of the top scuba diving areas in the United States. Scuba divers come to see more than 40 types of coral and 400 kinds of fish.

Florida also has more than 120 state parks for tourists to enjoy. Look at the map on this page to see the locations of some of our state parks. In the north, near Pensacola, is Big Lagoon State Park. People enjoy boating, fishing, camping, and hiking in this park. In the south is John Pennekamp Coral Reef State Park at Key Largo. Pennekamp Park has more visitors than any other state park in Florida.

Nancy Nehring / Getty Images

An egret in the Everglades ▶

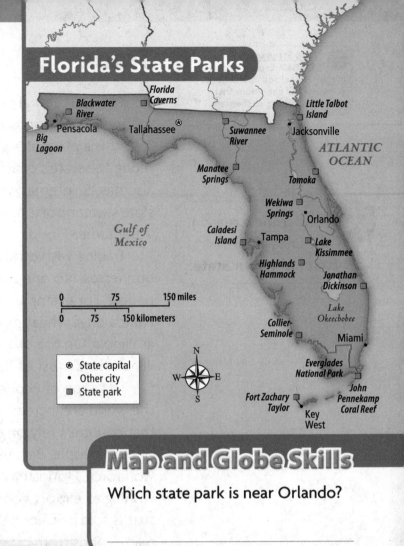

Florida's State Parks

Blackwater River
Florida Caverns
Pensacola
Tallahassee ⊛
Suwannee River
Little Talbot Island
Jacksonville
Big Lagoon
ATLANTIC OCEAN
Manatee Springs
Tomoka
Wekiwa Springs
Orlando
Gulf of Mexico
Caladesi Island
Tampa
Lake Kissimmee
Highlands Hammock
Jonathan Dickinson
Lake Okeechobee
Collier-Seminole
Miami
Everglades National Park
Fort Zachary Taylor
John Pennekamp Coral Reef
Key West

0   75   150 miles
0   75   150 kilometers

⊛ State capital
• Other city
▪ State park

N W E S

Map and Globe Skills

Which state park is near Orlando?

_____

Write a short essay about why tourism is important to our state.

_____

_____

_____

_____

_____

_____

_____

NGSS Standards
SS.4.E.1.2 Explain Florida's role in the national and international economy and conditions that attract businesses to the state.

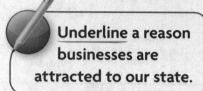

Underline a reason businesses are attracted to our state.

Trade

How do agricultural products and other goods get from Florida to other parts of the country and the world? One way is through ports. A port is a place along a coast where boats and ships can dock safely. Along the state's coastline, Florida has 14 deepwater ports. Florida also has 15 international airports that move goods every day. Our state's water ports and airports are another reason businesses are attracted to Florida.

Trading with other states and countries is important to Florida's businesses. No one place can meet all of the needs and wants of its people. For example, wheat does not grow well in Florida. Therefore, Florida buys wheat products from states that do grow wheat, such as Illinois. On the other hand, oranges do not grow well in Illinois, so Illinois buys most of its oranges from Florida.

This type of economic trade means that states and places around the world are increasingly **interdependent**, or connected. This means that countries rely on each other to meet the needs and wants of their people. Because of Florida's location, ports, and diverse workforce, Florida has become a major gateway for companies wishing to **export** goods to global markets. An export is something that is sold or traded to another country. Likewise, Florida **imports** many goods from other countries. An import is something that is brought in from another country for sale or use.

▼ The Port of Miami

Image Source / Getty Images

194

Florida's Economy

Use these words to complete the paragraph.

exports	technology	economy
Disney's	agriculture	phosphate

Florida plays a large role in the national and international

_____. The state provides goods and

services to other places. For example, Florida mines a lot of

_____. This product helps farmers around the

country and the world grow their crops. Other places use Florida's space

_____ too. Walt _____

resort has inspired other resorts and theme parks around the world. The

_____ industry helps feed people around the world.

The money Florida earns from these _____ allows

it to buy the goods and services it needs. By buying these products from

other places, Florida helps support the economies of other places.

Lesson 2

 Essential Question   How does the economy affect a people?

_____

_____

_____

Go back to _Show As You Go!_ on pages 174–175. ≪≪≪

Lesson 3 Florida's Government

? Essential Question

Why do people form governments?

What do you think?

_____

_____

_____

_____

_____

Words To Know

Look at the words below. Tell a partner what you know about these words.

*declaration

checks and balances

legislative branch

executive branch

judicial branch

NGSS Standards
SS.4.C.1.1 Describe how Florida's constitution protects the rights of citizens and provides for the structure, function and purpose of state government.
SS.4.C.3.1 Identify the three branches (Legislative, Judicial, Executive) of government in Florida and the powers of each.

196

Does your class have a class contract or constitution? These documents usually explain the rules that everyone has to follow. Write some of the rules in your classroom below.

_____

_____

_____

Like a classroom constitution, Florida's constitution describes the rules that the government has to follow. It is the plan for our state and local governments, and it describes how the government is set up. In 1968 members of Florida's government wrote the constitution we use today. This constitution protects the rights of citizens and explains the purpose of state government.

▲ The Florida state flag

The Florida State Capitol ▼

(t) Photodisc / Alamy; (b) Photodisc / Getty Images

State Government

Our state constitution has 12 separate sections called articles. Article One is called the **Declaration** of Rights. These rights are similar to our national Constitution's Bill of Rights. These rights include freedom of speech, freedom of the press, and freedom of religion. The Declaration of Rights states that the people are the source of the government's power and that "all natural persons, female and male alike, are equal before the law. . . ."

Like the U.S. Constitution, Florida's state constitution divides the government into three separate branches—legislative, executive, and judicial. Each branch has some power over the other two branches. This system is called **checks and balances**. A system of checks and balances makes sure that no one person or group gains too much power.

Reading Skill

Explain Author's Purpose

1. What did the writers of Florida's constitution want to accomplish?

   _____

   _____

   _____

2. Describe how Florida's constitution protects the rights of citizens.

   _____

   _____

Florida's Three Branches of Government

✏️ Underline the power of each branch of government.

◀ The legislative branch meets in the capitol.

The **legislative branch** makes the laws for our state. It has two parts—the Senate and the House of Representatives. The Senate has 40 members, who are called senators. The 120 members of the House of Representatives are called state representatives.

◀ The governor's mansion

The **executive branch** of government makes sure that the state laws are carried out. The people of Florida elect a governor to lead the executive branch.

◀ The Florida Supreme Court building

The **judicial branch** of government makes the meaning of laws clear. The Florida Supreme Court is the highest court in the state. It decides if laws passed by the legislative branch follow the rules of the state constitution.

NGSS Standards
SS.4.C.2.1 Discuss public issues in Florida that impact the daily lives of its citizens.
SS.4.C.3.2 Distinguish between state (governor, state representative, or senator) and local government (mayor, city commissioner).

Local Government

There are two types of local government in Florida: county government and municipal government. County governments run counties, and municipal governments run cities and towns.

Both forms of local government may have a legislative branch. These branches are called commissions or councils at the local level. Both forms of local government may also have an executive branch. Local governments in Florida call the head of the executive branch a mayor or city commissioner. In local government in Florida, only counties have a judicial branch.

Local governments provide a lot of services for Floridians. For example, municipal governments provide police and fire services. They also pick up garbage and maintain parks. County governments are in charge of running hospitals, holding elections, and maintaining highways.

County government is also responsible for providing education. Schools are required to provide a high quality education to all students. This is called school accountability. Schools in Florida are given a rating based on how their students do on tests. You can find the rating of your school on the Internet.

DID YOU KNOW?

To pay for the services of government, Floridians pay taxes. Taxes are money that people pay to support their government. Taxes can be raised in many different ways. Oftentimes, when you buy something, a percentage of what you pay goes to taxes.

THINK · PAIR · SHARE

Discuss with a partner how school accountability or taxes impact your life. Then share your ideas with another pair.

Students boarding a school bus (left) and students learning social studies (above).

(l) Comstock/PictureQuest, (r) Image Source/Alamy

Florida's Government

Use these words to complete these statements about Florida's state and local government.

governor   rights   constitution
judicial   mayor   local

1. A city commissioner or a _____ runs the executive branch of a city.

2. Florida's _____ divides the government into three branches of government.

3. Cities, towns, and counties are part of _____ government.

4. The _____ branch of government has the power to decide if laws passed by the legislature follow the rules of the state constitution.

5. The Florida constitution protects the _____ of citizens and provides for the purpose of state government.

6. The head of the executive branch of the state government is called the

   _____.

Lesson 3

 Essential Question   Why do people form governments?

_____

_____

_____

Go back to _Show As You Go!_ on pages 174–175.

  **There's More Online!**
● Games ● Assessments

Citizenship in Action

(?) Essential Question

How do people affect society?

What do you think?

_____

_____

_____

_____

Words To Know

Pick a symbol that shows how much you know about the meaning of the word. Draw the symbol next to the word.

? = I have no idea!
▲ = I know a little.
★ = I know a lot.

_____ **recycle**

_____ **petition**

_____ **conservation**

_____ ***consequences**

_____ **budget**

NGSS Standards
SS.4.C.2.1 Discuss public issues in Florida that impact the daily lives of its citizens.
SS.4.C.2.2 Identify ways citizens work together to influence government and help solve community and state problems.
SS.4.C.2.3 Explain the importance of public service, voting, and volunteerism.

Working together with other people is a great way to solve problems. How have you worked with someone to fix a problem? Explain below.

_____

_____

_____

_____

In this lesson, you'll read about how Ruby worked with others to solve a problem in her community.

Ruby is a fourth-grade student at Washington Elementary School. She saw a problem in a park in her town. People were throwing empty plastic bottles and aluminum cans in the trash cans. Ruby knew that this was wasteful and bad for the environment. She thought people should **recycle** these items instead. To recycle means to make something new from something that has been used before. Ruby wanted to fix this problem, so she decided to try to start a recycling program in her town's parks.

Read about Ruby and fill in the blank.

Hi! I'm Ruby. I care about the environment, and I want everyone to

_____.

Starting a Recycling Program

Ruby's town already had a recycling program for homes and businesses. But there were no recycling bins in the parks. Ruby asked her teacher for advice about how to start a recycling program for the parks. Her teacher told her to start a **petition** to show to the town council. A petition is a formal request made to a person of authority. It is usually made up of a list of people who support an idea to bring change. Ruby's teacher also told her that American citizens have the right to petition the government in order to change things and fix problems.

Ruby did some research about the importance of recycling before she started her petition. She looked up recycling on the Internet and read all about **conservation**. She found out that conservation is the protection and careful use of natural resources. She also learned that recycling not only conserves natural resources but also saves energy needed to create new items. Ruby thought it was amazing that recycling one aluminum can saves enough energy to power a television for two hours!

Ruby knew that she'd need help with her petition, so she asked her friends to volunteer. She shared her research about recycling and told them how important it is to recycle. Before she knew it, she had 20 volunteers helping her collect signatures for her petition!

DID YOU KNOW?
Many kinds of materials can be recycled. Paper, glass, metals, and plastics can all be made into products people can use.

Circle how recycling helps the environment. Underline how people can work together to influence government.

▼ Recycling bins in a park

PAPER   PLASTIC   METAL   GLASS   FOOD   OTHERS

▲ Voting makes our government strong.

Ruby Meets the Town Council

Over the next month, Ruby and the volunteers collected signatures for the petition. Once they had 5,000 signatures, Ruby delivered the petition to the town council. The clerk told her the petition would be discussed at the next meeting. Ruby wanted to explain her petition to the council members. When Ruby asked the clerk if she could speak at the meeting, the clerk said, "All town council meetings are open to the public. Anyone who wants to speak at the meeting can."

Ruby was very nervous about speaking before the town council. She practiced her presentation many times, and at the meeting she gave her speech without a single problem! Ruby explained the **consequences** of not recycling. The council said they would debate her petition at the next council meeting.

Ruby and her friends attended the debate the following week. The main issue was money. Some council members were concerned the town would not be able to afford the new recycling bins. Other members thought the town could afford the bins.

Momentum Creative Group / Alamy

Create a poster that tells people about the importance of recycling.

One council member said, "I don't see the need for recycling bins in our parks. People and businesses have recycling services. Why do we need it in the parks? We don't have the money in the **budget** for this!" A budget is a plan for using money. All governments have budgets that keep track of money used to run the government. Ruby knew that they would need to find the money to pay for recycling bins in the budget.

Next, the council called for a vote on the petition. From her social studies lessons at school, Ruby knew that voting is a way that people make a choice. She was very interested in this vote.

Ruby was afraid that the council would not support her petition. A clerk read the results of the vote. Out of the nine council members, six voted for the recycling bins! When Ruby heard the result, she was beaming with excitement! Ruby and her friends had made a difference!

Circle the correct answer. When a person offers to help without pay they are called a

_____ .

A. student
B. judge
C. volunteer

Underline what voting is. Then describe a community problem you would like to solve.

_____

_____

NGSS Standards
SS.4.C.2.1 Discuss public issues in Florida that impact the daily lives of its citizens. **SS.4.C.2.2** Identify ways citizens work together to influence government and help solve community and state problems. **SS.4.C.2.3** Explain the importance of public service, voting, and volunteerism.

203

NGSS Standards
SS.4.C.2.2 Identify ways citizens work together to influence government and help solve community and state problems.
SS.4.C.2.3 Explain the importance of public service, voting, and volunteerism.

Ruby Meets the Mayor

The day after the council approved the recycling bins, the mayor called Ruby! She thanked Ruby and her friends for working hard on the petition. She was very impressed with their work and told Ruby what good citizens she and her friends were. Ruby was so excited! She had an idea. "Would you like to come to my school and give a speech about being a good citizen?" Ruby asked. The mayor agreed.

The mayor talked to the entire school. She stressed the important things Ruby and her friends did and even gave them a plaque that said, "In appreciation of your public service." Public service is what people do to help their community. Firefighters, police officers, and teachers all provide a public service, as do people who volunteer at a senior center or food bank. Ruby and her friends provided a public service by making life better for everyone in their community.

Soon recycling bins appeared in the parks in Ruby's town. Every time Ruby sees one, she feels very proud! Ruby learned that when people work together, they can solve problems!

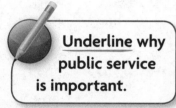

DID YOU KNOW?
Each person in the United States uses paper and wood products equal to about one 100-foot-tall Douglas fir tree per year.

Underline why public service is important.

204-205 (bkgd) Digital Vision/PunchStock

Public Issues

Think about a problem in your community or state. How could you work with others to solve this problem?

Problem: _____

Things I can do	Things I can do with others

Lesson 4

 Essential Question How do people affect society?

_____

_____

_____

_____

_____

_____

Go back to *Show As You Go!* on pages 174–175.

networks
There's More Online!
● Games ● Assessment

**Fill in the blanks with the missing word in the sentences below.
Then use the letters from the circles to answer the riddle.**

1. ⭘ _ _ _ _ ⭘ _ _ is an important mineral in Florida.

2. The _ _ _ _ _ _ ⭘ branch decides if laws follow the Florida constitution.

3. A ⭘ _ _ _ _ is a leader in the executive branch of local government.

4. Recycling helps the _ _ _ _ _ _ _ _ _ _ ⭘.

5. The business of buying and selling goods is called _ ⭘ _ _ ⭘.

6. The _ _ _ _ ⭘ program is run by NASA.

What kind of tree could grow in your hand?   a _ _ _ _ _   _ _ _ _ _

image100/CORBIS

FLORIDA

Read each statement below. If the statement is true, color
the corresponding letter above green. If the statement is false,
color the corresponding letter blue. The first one has been done for you.

F Tourists come to Florida to visit the Everglades.

L Florida's constitution lets the government do whatever it wants.

O Florida grows a lot of wheat.

R Florida's government has three branches.

I Citizens can work together by recycling.

D Immigrants have influenced Florida with their cultures.

A A budget is a plan for getting to school.

Unit Project

Hold a debate on a current public issue that affects citizens in Florida. Your debate will inform citizens about important issues. With a small group, choose a public issue. Research both sides of the issue and assign group members to sides. Before you begin working, look back at **Show As You Go!** on pages 174–175 to review your notes. Also read the list below to see what information should be included in your debate. As you work, check off each item as you include it.

Your debate should...   **Yes, it does!**

be based on your research. ☐

present both sides of the public issue. ☐

be persuasive and try to convince listeners to support one side of the issue. ☐

include all group members. ☐

Think about the Big Idea

BIG IDEA 💡 **Culture influences the way people live.**

What did you learn in this unit that helps you understand the BIG IDEA?

_____

_____

_____

_____

imagenavi/Getty Images

Read the passage "My Trip to Kennedy Space Center" and then answer Numbers 1 and 2.

My Trip to Kennedy Space Center

1 LAST spring, my family and I went to the Kennedy Space Center. I had a blast! Kennedy Space Center has been the site of many "firsts" in space. In 1961 the first American rocketed into space from Cape Canaveral (that's the location of the space center). In 1969 the first men to go to the moon blasted off from there.

2 I also learned that the National Aeronautics and Space Administration (or NASA for short) was created in 1958. Its creation was part of the space race. The space race was a competition between our nation and the Soviet Union to see which country could get to the moon first.

3 We took a bus tour around the whole space center. The tour stops at the Launch Complex 39 Observation Gantry. It is a big observation deck that you can walk onto and look out. You get to see the launch pad and almost the entire complex. It is so cool!

4 Next on the bus tour was the Apollo/Saturn V Center. It has some great displays. I liked the spacesuits the best. Next we saw the rocket display and the capsules. That was really cool too! The space center also shows a film that recreates a launch that is very realistic.

5 One of the last stops on the tour was the International Space Station Center. Here visitors can walk through capsules. You can also visit the Astronaut Hall of Fame. It includes a history of the space program and information about the astronauts who have launched from Kennedy Space Center. I learned so much about the space program during our visit!

"My Trip to Kennedy Space Center" property of McGraw-Hill Education.

GO ON →

Now answer Numbers 1 and 2. Base your answers on the passage "My Trip to Kennedy Space Center."

1 This question has two parts. First, answer Part A. Then, answer Part B.

Part A What is the author's MAIN purpose for writing "My Trip to Kennedy Space Center"?

(A) to tell where NASA is located

(B) to tell about the moon landing

(C) to tell the reasons for the space race

(D) to tell about his trip to the Kennedy Space Center

Part B Which sentence supports your answer in Part A?

(A) "It is a big observation deck that you can walk onto and look out." (paragraph 3)

(B) "It includes a history of the space program and information about the astronauts who have launched from Kennedy Space Center." (paragraph 5)

(C) "I learned so much about the space program during our visit!" (paragraph 5)

(D) "I had a blast!" (paragraph 1)

2 Read this sentence from the passage.

"It is a big observation deck that you can walk onto and look out."

What does the word <u>observation</u> mean?

(A) the act of looking aside

(B) the act of being noticed

(C) the act of noticing

(D) the act of walking

GO ONLINE to connected.mcgraw-hill.com for enhanced Florida Test Preparation options, available through Engrade.

Reference Section

Geography and You

Geography is the study of Earth and the people, plants, and animals that live on it. Most people think of geography as learning about cities, states, and countries, but geography is far more. Geography includes learning about land, such as mountains and plains, and bodies of water, such as oceans, lakes, and rivers.

Geography includes the study of how people adapt to living in a new place. Geography is also about how people move around, how they move goods, and how ideas travel from place to place.

Dictionary of Geographic Terms

1 **BAY** Body of water partly surrounded by land

2 **BEACH** Land covered with sand or pebbles next to an ocean or lake

3 **CANAL** Waterway dug across the land to connect two bodies of water

4 **CANYON** Deep river valley with steep sides

5 **CLIFF** High steep face of rock

6 **COAST** Land next to an ocean

7 **DESERT** A dry environment with few plants and animals

8 **GULF** Body of water partly surrounded by land; larger than a bay

9 **HARBOR** Protected place by an ocean or river where ships can safely stay

10 **HILL** Rounded, raised landform; not as high as a mountain

11 **ISLAND** Land that is surrounded on all sides by water

12 LAKE Body of water completely surrounded by land

13 MESA Landform that looks like a high, flat table

14 MOUNTAIN High landform with steep sides; higher than a hill

15 OCEAN Large body of salt water

16 PENINSULA Land that has water on all sides but one

17 PLAIN Large area of flat land

18 PLATEAU High flat area that rises steeply above the surrounding land

19 PORT Place where ships load and unload goods

20 RIVER Long stream of water that empties into another body of water

21 VALLEY Area of low land between hills or mountains

Florida: Political

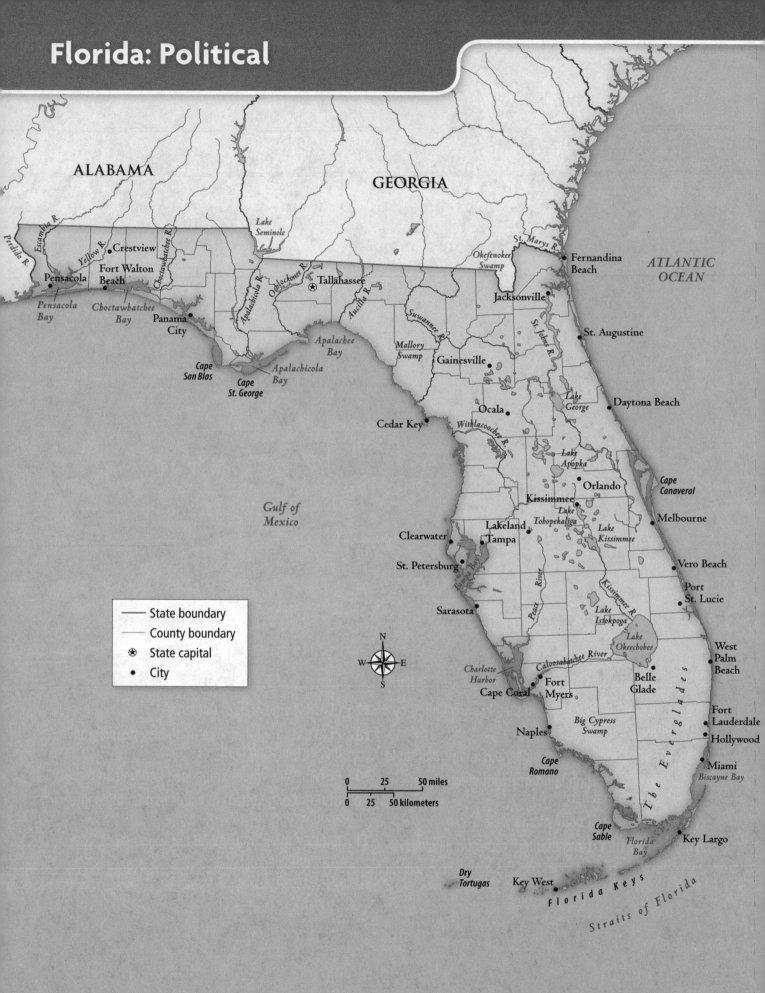

ALABAMA

GEORGIA

ATLANTIC OCEAN

Perdido R.

Escambia R.

Yellow R.

Crestview

Choctawhatchee R.

Lake Seminole

Fort Walton Beach

Pensacola

Pensacola Bay

Choctawhatchee Bay

Panama City

Apalachicola R.

Ochlockonee R.

Tallahassee

Aucilla R.

Suwannee R.

Okefenokee Swamp

St. Marys R.

Fernandina Beach

Jacksonville

St. Augustine

Apalachee Bay

Cape San Blas

Apalachicola Bay

Cape St. George

Mallory Swamp

Gainesville

St. Johns R.

Lake George

Daytona Beach

Cedar Key

Withlacoochee R.

Ocala

Lake Apopka

Cape Canaveral

Gulf of Mexico

Orlando

Lake Tohopekaliga

Melbourne

Kissimmee

Lake Kissimmee

Clearwater

Lakeland

Tampa

Vero Beach

St. Petersburg

Tampa Bay

Peace River

Port St. Lucie

Sarasota

Kissimmee R.

Lake Istokpoga

West Palm Beach

Lake Okeechobee

Charlotte Harbor

Caloosahatchee River

Belle Glade

Fort Lauderdale

Cape Coral

Fort Myers

The Everglades

Hollywood

Naples

Big Cypress Swamp

Cape Romano

Miami

Biscayne Bay

	State boundary
	County boundary
✪	State capital
•	City

N
W E
S

Cape Sable

Florida Bay

Key Largo

Dry Tortugas

Key West

Florida Keys

Straits of Florida

0   25   50 miles
0   25   50 kilometers

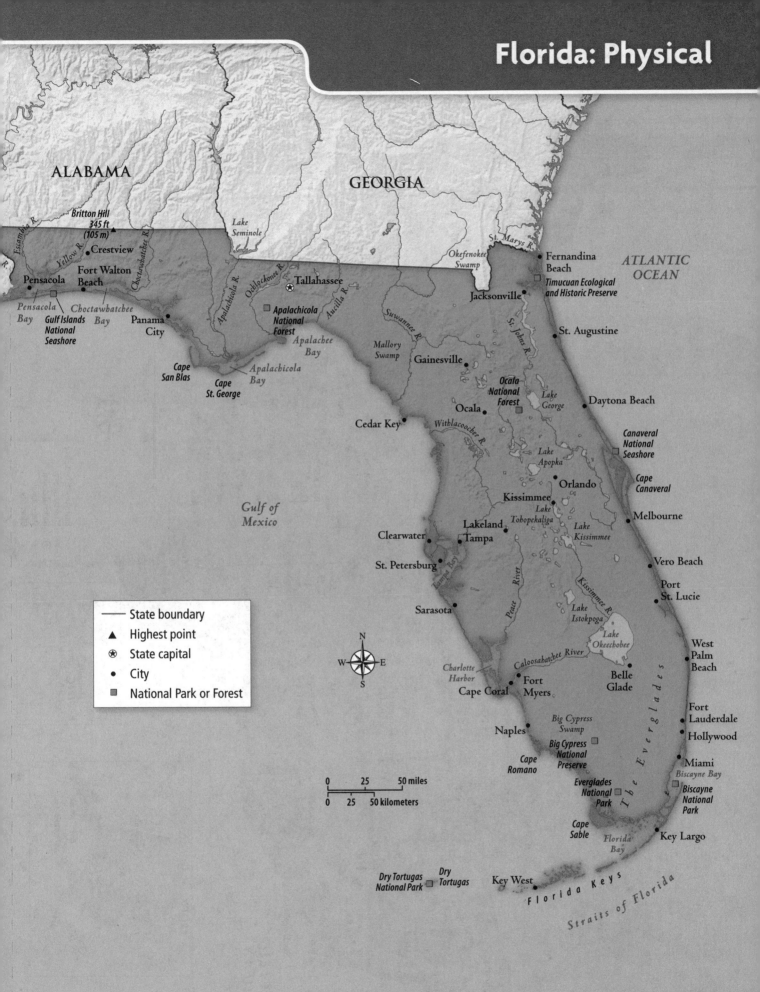

ALABAMA

GEORGIA

Britton Hill
345 ft
(105 m) ▲

Crestview

Fort Walton
Beach

Pensacola

Pensacola
Bay

Gulf Islands
National
Seashore

Choctawhatchee
Bay

Panama
City

Cape
San Blas

Cape
St. George

Escambia R.

Yellow R.

Choctawhatchee R.

Apalachicola R.

Ochlockonee R.

Lake
Seminole

Tallahassee

Apalachicola
National
Forest

Aucilla R.

*Apalachee
Bay*

*Apalachicola
Bay*

Okefenokee
Swamp

St. Marys R.

Fernandina
Beach

Timucuan Ecological
and Historic Preserve

Jacksonville

St. Augustine

ATLANTIC
OCEAN

Suwannee R.

Mallory
Swamp

Gainesville

Ocala
National
Forest

Ocala

St. Johns R.

Lake
George

Daytona Beach

Cedar Key

Withlacoochee R.

Lake
Apopka

Orlando

Kissimmee

Lake
Tohopekaliga

Canaveral
National
Seashore

Cape
Canaveral

Melbourne

Lake
Kissimmee

Vero Beach

Port
St. Lucie

*Gulf of
Mexico*

Clearwater

Tampa

St. Petersburg

Tampa Bay

Lakeland

Peace River

Kissimmee R.

Lake
Istokpoga

Sarasota

Lake
Okeechobee

West
Palm
Beach

*Charlotte
Harbor*

Cape Coral

Fort
Myers

Caloosahatchee River

Belle
Glade

The Everglades

Fort
Lauderdale

Hollywood

Naples

*Big Cypress
Swamp*

Big Cypress
National
Preserve

Cape
Romano

Everglades
National
Park

Cape
Sable

*Florida
Bay*

Miami

Biscayne Bay

Biscayne
National
Park

Key Largo

Dry Tortugas
National Park

*Dry
Tortugas*

Key West

Florida Keys

Straits of Florida

Legend

— State boundary
▲ Highest point
✪ State capital
• City
◻ National Park or Forest

N
W E
S

| 0 | 25 | 50 miles |
| 0 | 25 | 50 kilometers |

United States: Political

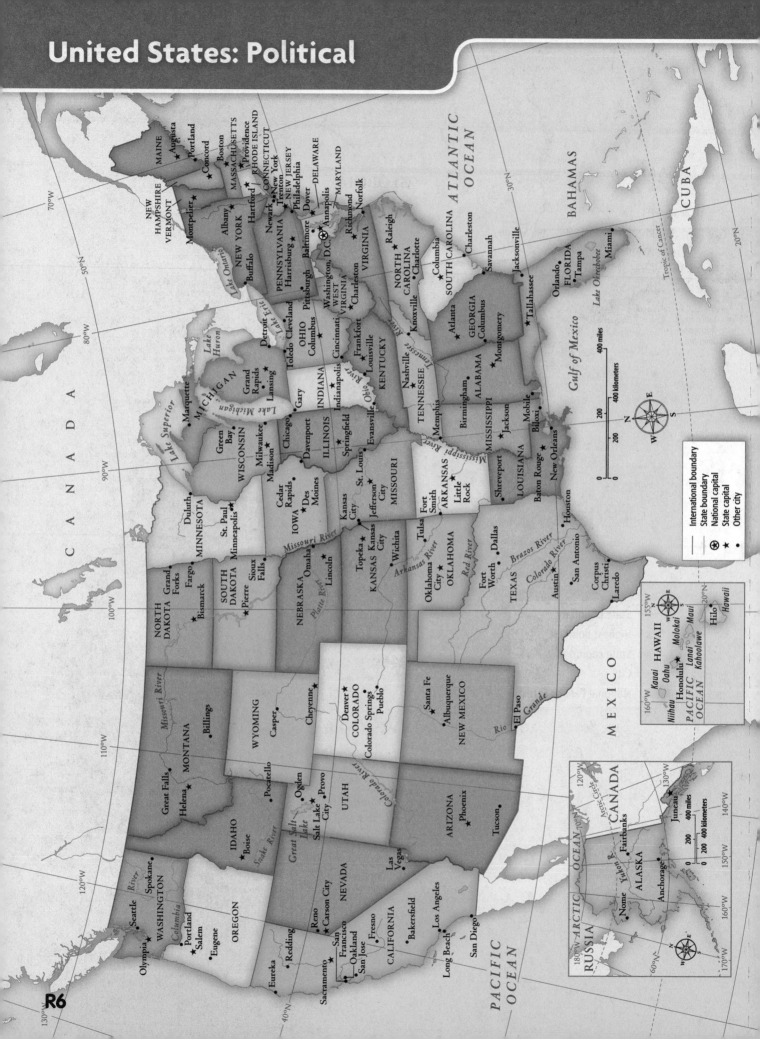

United States: Physical

Legend
- Interational boundary
- State boundary
- ⊛ National capital
- ▲ Mountain peak
- ▲ Highest point
- ▶ Lowest point

ATLANTIC OCEAN

BAHAMA

CUBA

Straits of Florida

Florida Keys

Lake Okeechobee

FL

GA

Chattahoochee R.

Gulf of Mexico

Mississippi River Delta

Mobile Bay

GULF COASTAL PLAIN

Tropic of Cancer

MEXICO

LA

MS

AL

Alabama River

TN

Mt. Mitchell 6,684 ft. (2,037 m) ▲

SC

NC

Savannah R.

ATLANTIC COASTAL PLAIN

PIEDMONT

APPALACHIAN MOUNTAINS

Tennessee River

KY

VA

WV

Cape Hatteras

Chesapeake Bay

MD DE Delaware Bay

Washington, D.C. ⊛

NJ

PA

ALLEGHENY PLATEAU

ALLEGHENY MOUNTAINS

NY

ADIRONDACK MOUNTAINS

Lake Ontario

Lake Erie

OH

Ohio River

IN

Wabash

IL

Lake Michigan

MI

Lake Huron

Lake Superior

GREAT LAKES

CANADA

Hudson R.

St. Lawrence R.

ME

Cape Cod

NH

MA

VT

GREEN MOUNTAINS

Mt. Washington 6,288 ft. (1,917 m)

CT RI

Long Island

WI

MN

MESABI RANGE

Lake of the Woods

Mississippi River

IA

CENTRAL PLAINS

MO

INTERIOR PLAINS

OZARK PLATEAU

Arkansas River

OUACHITA MOUNTAINS

AR

Red River

OK

Missouri River

NE

Platte River

KS

Brazos River

TX

Colorado River

EDWARDS PLATEAU

Pecos River

Rio Grande

Gulf of California

SONORAN DESERT

Gila River

AZ

Humphreys Peak 12,633 ft. (3,851 m) ▲

CONTINENTAL DIVIDE

NM

Guadalupe Peak 8,749 ft. (2,667 m) ▲

Wheeler Peak 13,161 ft. (4,011 m) ▲

Pikes Peak 14,110 ft. (4,301 m) ▲

CO

COLORADO PLATEAU

Mt. Elbert 14,433 ft. (4,399 m) ▲

GREAT PLAINS

ND

SD

BLACK HILLS

WY

MT

Missouri River

Granite Peak 12,799 ft. (3,901 m) ▲

ROCKY MOUNTAINS

ID

Snake River

Columbia River

COLUMBIA PLATEAU

Kings Peak 13,528 ft. (4,123 m) ▲

WASATCH RANGE

UT

Great Salt Lake

GREAT SALT LAKE DESERT

GREAT BASIN

NV

Lake Tahoe

Lake Mead

Colorado River

MOJAVE DESERT

Salton Sea

Death Valley -282 ft. (-86 m) ▶

Mt. Whitney 14,494 ft. (4,418 m) ▲

SIERRA NEVADA

CENTRAL VALLEY

CA

Channel Islands

San Francisco Bay

Cape Mendocino

COAST RANGES

Mt. Shasta 14,162 ft. (4,317 m) ▲

Mt. Hood 11,239 ft. (3,426 m) ▲

OR

CASCADE RANGE

Mt. St. Helens 8,363 ft. (2,549 m) ▲

WA

Mt. Rainier 14,410 ft. (4,392 m) ▲

Puget Sound

Columbia R.

PACIFIC OCEAN

Scale
- 400 miles
- 400 kilometers
- 200
- 200
- 0
- 0

Hawaii inset
HAWAII

Kauai

Niihau

Oahu

Molokai

Maui

Lanai

Kahoolawe

Hawaii

Mauna Kea 13,796 ft. (4,205 m) ▲

PACIFIC OCEAN

- 200 miles
- 200 kilometers
- 100
- 100
- 0
- 0

Alaska inset
ARCTIC OCEAN

RUSSIA

Bering Strait

Aleutian Islands

Bering Sea

ALASKA

BROOKS RANGE

Arctic Circle

Yukon River

CANADA

ALASKA RANGE

Mt. McKinley 20,320 ft. (6,194 m) ▲

Gulf of Alaska

- 400 miles
- 400 kilometers
- 200
- 200
- 0
- 0

30°N · 40°N · 50°N · 60°N · 70°N · 20°N

70°W · 80°W · 90°W · 100°W · 110°W · 120°W · 130°W · 140°W · 150°W · 160°W · 170°W

155°W · 160°W · 20°N

North America: Political

ASIA

EUROPE

North Pole

ARCTIC
OCEAN

*Lincoln
Sea*

*Greenland
Sea*

ICELAND

*Chukchi
Sea*

GREENLAND
(Denmark)

*Bering
Sea*

*Beaufort
Sea*

*Baffin
Bay*

Bering Strait

AK
(U.S.)

YUKON

NORTHWEST
TERRITORIES

NUNAVUT

Davis Strait

*Gulf of
Alaska*

*Labrador
Sea*

*Hudson
Bay*

NEWFOUNDLAND
AND LABRADOR

CANADA

BRITISH
COLUMBIA

ALBERTA

MANITOBA

SASKATCHEWAN

QUÉBEC

ONTARIO

PRINCE EDWARD
ISLAND

NOVA SCOTIA

WA

MT

ND

MN

Ottawa ⊛

ME

NEW BRUNSWICK

OR

ID

SD

WI

MI

NY

VT
NH
MA
RI
CT

UNITED STATES

WY

NE

IA

IL

IN

OH

PA

NJ
DE
MD

ATLANTIC
OCEAN

NV

UT

CO

KS

MO

WV

VA

Washington, D.C. ⊛

CA

AZ

NM

OK

AR

KY

TN

NC

SC

BERMUDA
(U.K.)

MS

AL

GA

TX

LA

FL

THE
BAHAMAS

PACIFIC
OCEAN

Gulf of California

Gulf of Mexico

DOMINICAN
REPUBLIC

PUERTO
RICO
(U.S.)

ST. KITTS
AND NEVIS

ANTIGUA
AND
BARBUDA

CUBA

MEXICO

DOMINICA

ST. LUCIA

| 0 | 250 | 500 miles |

| 0 | 250 | 500 kilometers |

Mexico City ⊛

JAMAICA

HAITI

Caribbean Sea

ST. VINCENT &
THE GRENADINES

BARBADOS

GRENADA

BELIZE

HONDURAS

TRINIDAD AND
TOBAGO

GUATEMALA

NICARAGUA

EL SALVADOR

COSTA RICA

SOUTH
AMERICA

PANAMA

Equator

— International boundary

— State boundary

⊛ National capital

N
W E
S

R8

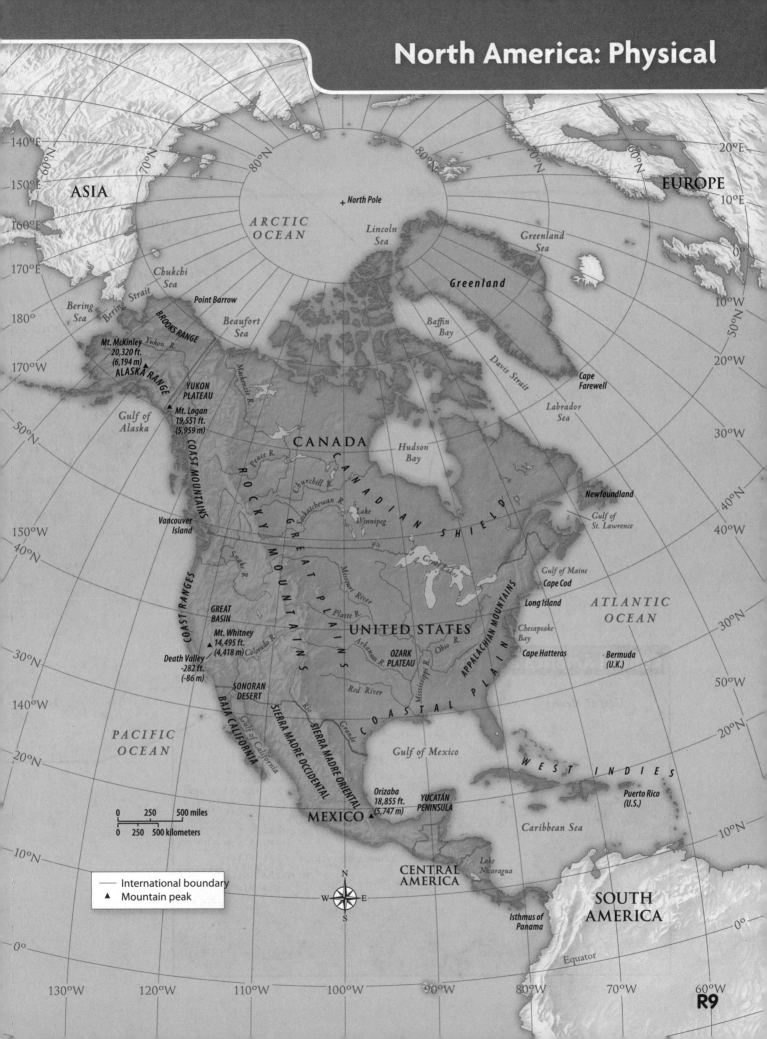

North America: Physical

ASIA

EUROPE

140°E 60°N 70°N 80°N 80°N 60°N 20°E
150°E 10°E
160°E ARCTIC + North Pole 0°
170°E OCEAN Lincoln Greenland 80°N
Sea Sea 10°W
Chukchi 70°N
180° Sea Point Barrow Greenland 60°N
Bering Beaufort Baffin
170°W Sea BROOKS RANGE Sea Bay Davis Strait 20°W
Mt. McKinley Yukon R.
20,320 ft. Cape
(6,194 m) ALASKA RANGE Farewell
YUKON Mackenzie R. Labrador 30°W
PLATEAU Mt. Logan Sea
Gulf of 19,551 ft. CANADA Hudson
Alaska (5,959 m) Peace R. Bay
Churchill R. Newfoundland 40°N
Vancouver Saskatchewan R. Lake Gulf of
Island Winnipeg St. Lawrence 40°W
150°W Missouri Gulf of Maine
40°N Snake R. River Great Lakes Cape Cod
GREAT Platte R. Long Island ATLANTIC
BASIN UNITED STATES Chesapeake OCEAN 30°N
Mt. Whitney Colorado R. Arkansas R. Bay
14,495 ft. OZARK Ohio R. Cape Hatteras Bermuda
30°N (4,418 m) PLATEAU (U.K.)
Death Valley Red River 50°W
-282 ft.
(-86 m) SONORAN
DESERT Rio COASTAL PLAIN 20°N
140°W Gulf of Grande
California
PACIFIC Gulf of Mexico WEST INDIES
20°N OCEAN Orizaba Puerto Rico
18,855 ft. YUCATÁN (U.S.)
250 500 miles (5,747 m) PENINSULA 10°N
0 MEXICO Caribbean Sea
0 250 500 kilometers CENTRAL Lake
10°N AMERICA Nicaragua
—— International boundary N SOUTH
▲ Mountain peak W E AMERICA
S Isthmus of
Panama 0°
0° Equator
130°W 120°W 110°W 100°W 90°W 80°W 70°W 60°W

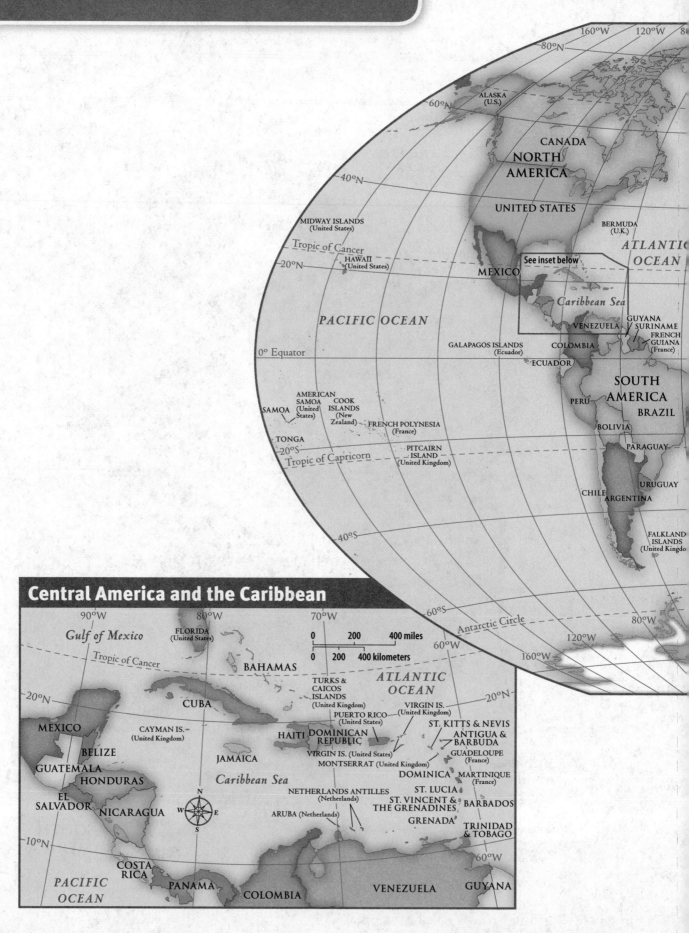

ALASKA
(U.S.)

CANADA

NORTH
AMERICA

UNITED STATES

BERMUDA
(U.K.)

MIDWAY ISLANDS
(United States)

ATLANTIC
OCEAN

Tropic of Cancer

HAWAII
(United States)

See inset below

MEXICO

Caribbean Sea

VENEZUELA

GUYANA
SURINAME
FRENCH
GUIANA
(France)

PACIFIC OCEAN

GALAPAGOS ISLANDS
(Ecuador)

COLOMBIA

0° Equator

ECUADOR

SOUTH
AMERICA

PERU

BRAZIL

AMERICAN
SAMOA
(United
States)

COOK
ISLANDS
(New
Zealand)

BOLIVIA

SAMOA

FRENCH POLYNESIA
(France)

PARAGUAY

TONGA

20°S

PITCAIRN
ISLAND
(United Kingdom)

URUGUAY

Tropic of Capricorn

CHILE

ARGENTINA

40°S

FALKLAND
ISLANDS
(United Kingdo

60°S

Antarctic Circle

80°W

120°W

160°W

Central America and the Caribbean

Gulf of Mexico

FLORIDA
(United States)

0   200   400 miles

0   200   400 kilometers

Tropic of Cancer

BAHAMAS

ATLANTIC
OCEAN

20°N

TURKS &
CAICOS
ISLANDS
(United Kingdom)

CUBA

VIRGIN IS.
(United Kingdom)

20°N

PUERTO RICO
(United States)

MEXICO

CAYMAN IS.
(United Kingdom)

HAITI

DOMINICAN
REPUBLIC

ST. KITTS & NEVIS

ANTIGUA &
BARBUDA

BELIZE

JAMAICA

VIRGIN IS. (United States)

GUADELOUPE
(France)

GUATEMALA

MONTSERRAT (United Kingdom)

HONDURAS

Caribbean Sea

DOMINICA

MARTINIQUE
(France)

EL
SALVADOR

NICARAGUA

N

NETHERLANDS ANTILLES
(Netherlands)

ST. LUCIA

ST. VINCENT &
THE GRENADINES

BARBADOS

W   E

ARUBA (Netherlands)

GRENADA

S

TRINIDAD
& TOBAGO

10°N

COSTA
RICA

PACIFIC
OCEAN

PANAMA

COLOMBIA

VENEZUELA

GUYANA

60°W

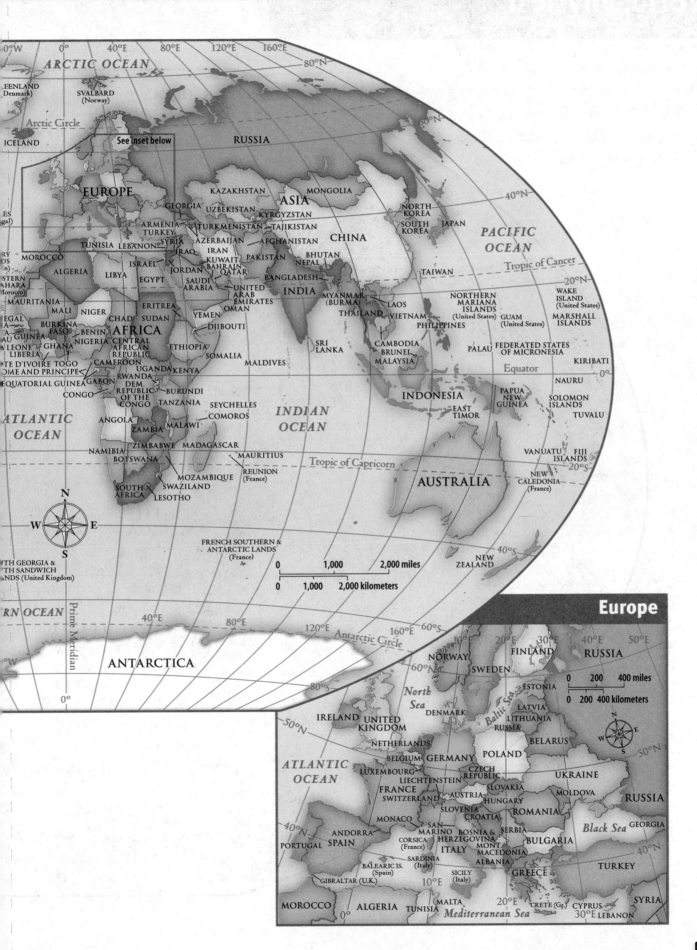

ARCTIC OCEAN

0°W 0° 40°E 80°E 120°E 160°E 80°N

GREENLAND
(Denmark)

SVALBARD
(Norway)

Arctic Circle

ICELAND

RUSSIA

60°N

EUROPE

See inset below

ES
(gal)

KAZAKHSTAN MONGOLIA ASIA 40°N

GEORGIA

UZBEKISTAN KYRGYZSTAN

RY
DS
(n)

ARMENIA
TURKEY

TURKMENISTAN TAJIKISTAN

NORTH
KOREA

SOUTH
KOREA JAPAN PACIFIC
OCEAN

MOROCCO TUNISIA LEBANON SYRIA
IRAQ AZERBAIJAN AFGHANISTAN CHINA

STERN
AHARA
(orocco)

ALGERIA LIBYA ISRAEL JORDAN
IRAN KUWAIT PAKISTAN NEPAL BHUTAN

TAIWAN Tropic of Cancer

BAHRAIN
EGYPT QATAR BANGLADESH 20°N

MAURITANIA SAUDI
ARABIA UNITED
ARAB INDIA MYANMAR
(BURMA) LAOS

NORTHERN
MARIANA
ISLANDS
(United States)

WAKE
ISLAND
(United States)

EGAL
MALI NIGER EMIRATES OMAN THAILAND VIETNAM GUAM
(United States)

MARSHALL
ISLANDS

AU GUINEA
LEONE BURKINA
FASO BENIN CHAD SUDAN ERITREA YEMEN DJIBOUTI

PHILIPPINES FEDERATED STATES
OF MICRONESIA

GHANA NIGERIA AFRICA CENTRAL
AFRICAN
REPUBLIC ETHIOPIA SRI
LANKA CAMBODIA PALAU KIRIBATI

TE D'IVOIRE TOGO
OME AND PRINCIPE CAMEROON UGANDA SOMALIA MALDIVES BRUNEI
MALAYSIA Equator 0°

EQUATORIAL GUINEA GABON RWANDA
DEM.
REPUBLIC
OF THE
CONGO KENYA BURUNDI INDONESIA PAPUA
NEW
GUINEA NAURU

CONGO TANZANIA SEYCHELLES EAST
TIMOR SOLOMON
ISLANDS TUVALU

ATLANTIC
OCEAN ANGOLA ZAMBIA MALAWI COMOROS INDIAN
OCEAN

NAMIBIA ZIMBABWE MADAGASCAR MAURITIUS Tropic of Capricorn VANUATU FIJI
ISLANDS 20°S

BOTSWANA REUNION
(France) AUSTRALIA NEW
CALEDONIA
(France)

N SOUTH
AFRICA MOZAMBIQUE
SWAZILAND
LESOTHO

W E

S

TH GEORGIA &
TH SANDWICH
NDS (United Kingdom)

FRENCH SOUTHERN &
ANTARCTIC LANDS
(France)

0   1,000   2,000 miles
0 1,000 2,000 kilometers

40°S

NEW
ZEALAND

RN OCEAN 40°E 80°E 120°E 160°E 60°S
Antarctic Circle

W 0°

ANTARCTICA

80°S

Prime Meridian

Europe

NORWAY FINLAND RUSSIA
60°N SWEDEN 0 200 400 miles
0 200 400 kilometers

North
Sea ESTONIA

IRELAND UNITED
KINGDOM DENMARK Baltic Sea LATVIA
LITHUANIA
RUSSIA

50°N NETHERLANDS BELARUS 50°N

BELGIUM GERMANY POLAND

ATLANTIC
OCEAN LUXEMBOURG CZECH
REPUBLIC UKRAINE

LIECHTENSTEIN
FRANCE SLOVAKIA
SWITZERLAND AUSTRIA HUNGARY MOLDOVA RUSSIA

MONACO SLOVENIA ROMANIA

40°N SAN
MARINO CROATIA Black Sea GEORGIA

ANDORRA CORSICA
(France) BOSNIA &
HERZEGOVINA SERBIA BULGARIA

PORTUGAL SPAIN ITALY MONT.
MACEDONIA 40°N

SARDINIA
(Italy) ALBANIA GREECE TURKEY

BALEARIC IS.
(Spain) SICILY
(Italy)

GIBRALTAR (U.K.) 10°E 20°E CRETE (Gr.) CYPRUS SYRIA
MOROCCO 0° ALGERIA TUNISIA MALTA Mediterranean Sea 30°E LEBANON

R11

World: Physical

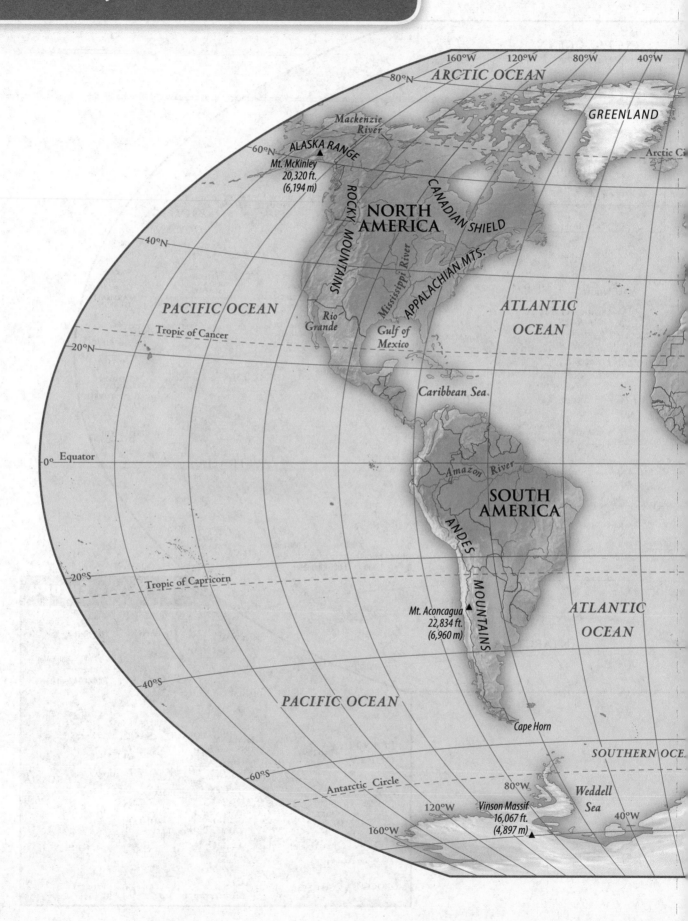

160°W 120°W 80°W 40°W

80°N ARCTIC OCEAN

GREENLAND

Mackenzie River

60°N ALASKA RANGE
Mt. McKinley
20,320 ft.
(6,194 m)

Arctic Ci

ROCKY MOUNTAINS

NORTH
AMERICA

CANADIAN SHIELD

Mississippi River

APPALACHIAN MTS.

40°N

PACIFIC OCEAN

ATLANTIC
OCEAN

Tropic of Cancer

Rio Grande

20°N

Gulf of
Mexico

Caribbean Sea

Amazon River

0° Equator

SOUTH
AMERICA

ANDES

20°S Tropic of Capricorn

MOUNTAINS

ATLANTIC
OCEAN

Mt. Aconcagua
22,834 ft.
(6,960 m)

40°S

PACIFIC OCEAN

Cape Horn

SOUTHERN OCE.

60°S

Antarctic Circle

80°W Weddell
Sea

120°W Vinson Massif
16,067 ft.
(4,897 m)

160°W

40°W

40°E 80°E 120°E 160°E
ARCTIC OCEAN
80°N

Lena
River
Yenisey River
Ob River
60°N
URAL MTS.
Volga River
Sea of Okhotsk

EUROPE
Caspian Sea
40°N
ALPS
ASIA
GOBI
Mont Blanc
Black Sea ▲ Mt. Elbrus
15,711 ft. 18,510 ft.
(4,807 m) (5,642 m)
HINDU KUSH
Chang River
Mediterranean Sea
HIMALAYA
Tropic of Cancer
SYRIAN
DESERT
Mt. Everest
20°N
Ganges River 29,035 ft.
S A H A R A (8,850 m)
Red Sea
DECCAN
Nile River PLATEAU
Arabian Bay of South Philippine
AFRICA Sea Bengal China Sea PACIFIC OCEAN
Sea
Congo River
Mt. Kilimanjaro
19,340 ft. Equator 0°
(5,895 m)

INDIAN
OCEAN
Coral
NAMIB DESERT Sea
KALAHARI GREAT 20°S
DESERT Tropic of Capricorn SANDY
DESERT
AUSTRALIA
Cape of Darling River
Good Hope Mt. Kosciuszko
N 7,310 ft.
(2,228 m)
W E 40°S
S

0 1,000 2,000 miles

0 1,000 2,000 kilometers

40°E 80°E 120°E 160°E
60°S
Antarctic Circle
ANTARCTICA

R13

Glossary

This Glossary will help you to pronounce and understand the meanings of the vocabulary terms in this book. The page number at the end of the definition tells where the term first appears. Words with an asterisk (*) before them are academic vocabulary words.

A

*abandon (uh • BAN • duhn) to leave or to give up on (p. 67)

abolitionist (a • buh • LIH • shuhn • ihst) a person who wanted to end slavery in the United States (p. 107)

*according (uh • KORD • ing) as reported or stated (p. 137)

*affect (uh • FEHKT) to influence or have an effect on (p. 16)

agriculture (A • grih • kuhl • chuhr) the farming of crops and the raising of animals (p. 73)

*alter (AWL • tuhr) to change (p. 166)

*approximately (uh • PRAHK • suh • muht • lee) near or close (p. 152)

*argue (AHR • gyuh) to disagree (p. 116)

*assemble (uh • SEHM • buhl) to put together (p. 104)

B

black codes (BLAK KOHDS) laws which restricted the rights of African Americans during Reconstruction (p. 116)

blockade (blah • KAYD) shutting off an area to keep people and supplies from going in and out (p. 110)

boom (BOOM) a rapid increase in economic growth (p. 144)

boycott (BOI • kaht) to refuse to do business with a person, group, company, or country (p. 166)

budget (BUH • juht) a plan for using money (p. 203)

bust (BUHST) period of financial ruin (p. 148)

C

cardinal directions (KAHR • duh • nuhl duh • REHK • shuhns) north, south, east, and west (p. 13)

cash crop (KASH KRAHP) a crop that is grown to be sold for profit (p. 99)

checks and balances (CHEHKS AND BA • luhnts • sehz) a system in government that makes sure that no one person or group of people can gain too much power (p. 197)

civil disobedience (SIH • vuhl dihs • uh • BEE • dee • uhnts) refusing to follow laws considered unfair in order to bring change (p. 165)

civil rights (SIH • vuhl RYTS) the rights of every citizen to be treated equally under the law (p. 163)

civil war (SIH • vuhl WAWR) a war among people who live in the same country (p. 109)

climate (KLY • muht) the pattern of weather in a certain place over a long period of time (p. 24)

colony (KAH • luh • nee) a place that is ruled by another country (p. 51)

compass rose (KUHM • puhs ROHZ) a symbol on a map that shows the cardinal and intermediate directions (p. 13)

*conduct (kahn • DUHKT) to guide (p. 110)

conquistador (kahn • KEES • tuh • dawr) an explorer from the European country of Spain (p. 49)

*consequence (KAHN • suh • kwents) the outcome of an action (p. 202)

conservation (kahn • suhr • VAY • shuhn) the protection and careful use of natural resources (p. 201)

constitution (kahn • stuh • TOO • shuhn) a written plan for government (p. 116)

convert (kuhn • VUHRT) to change your beliefs (p. 63)

culture (KUHL • chuhr) the way of life of a group of people (p. 29)

D

*debate (dih • BAYT) an argument (p. 107)

*declaration (deh • kluh • RAY • shuhn) the act of making something known (p. 197)

depression (dih • PREH • shuhn) a period of severe economic hardship with high unemployment (p. 149)

*develop (dih • VEHL • uhp) to create (p. 25)

Glossary

dictator (DIHK • tay • tuhr) a person with complete power over a country (p. 156)

discrimination (dihs • krih • muh • NAY • shuhn) an unfair difference in the way people are treated (p. 164)

***diverse** (deye • VUHRS) not all the same; varied (p. 188)

drought (DRAUT) a long period without rain (p. 26)

E

enlist (ihn • LIHST) to join a military service voluntarily (p. 157)

entrepreneur (ahn • truh • pruh • NUHR) a person who starts a business (p. 136)

ethnic group (ETH • nihk GROOP) a group of people from the same country or with a shared culture (p. 185)

executive branch (ihg • ZEH • kyuh • tihv BRANCH) the part of government that makes sure that laws are carried out (p. 197)

expedition (ehk • spuh • DIH • shuhn) a journey for a special purpose (p. 53)

export (ehk • SPAWRT) something that is sold or traded to another country (p. 194)

***expose** (ihk • SPOHZ) to put at risk (p. 75)

F

fertile (FUHR • tuhl) good for growing (p. 33)

ford (FORD) a shallow place where a river or stream may be crossed (p. 103)

***frequently** (FREE • kwuhnt • lee) often (p. 140)

G

***general** (JEH • nuh • ruhl) a high-ranking officer in the military (p. 71)

geography (jee • AH • gruh • fee) the study of Earth (p. 16)

Great Depression (GRAYT dih • PREH • shuhn) a time in the 1930s when people were poor and many did not have jobs (p. 150)

H

heritage (HEHR • uh • tihj) a way of life that has been handed down from the past (p. 184)

hurricane (HUHR • uh • kayn) a large, severe storm that brings heavy rainfall and strong winds (p. 27)

I

immigrant (IH • muh • gruhnt) a person who lives in a country in which he or she was not born (p. 135)

import (ihm • PORT) something that is brought in from another country for sale or use (p. 194)

independent (in • duh • PEN • duhnt) the state of being free (p. 141)

***indicate** (IN • duh • kayt) to suggest or to mean (p. 13)

industry (IHN • duhs • tree) all the businesses that make one kind of product or provide one kind of service (p. 133)

integration (in • tuh • GRAY • shuhn) the act of making something open to all people (p. 163)

interdependent (ihn • tuhr • dih • PEHN • duhnt) to depend on something or someone else (p. 194)

intermediate directions (ihn • tuhr • MEE • dee • uht duh • REHK • shuhns) the directions in between the cardinal directions; they include northeast, northwest, southeast, southwest (p. 13)

J

judicial branch (joo • DIH • shuhl BRANCH) the part of government that makes the meaning of laws clear (p. 197)

Glossary

L

landform (LAND • form) a shape of land on Earth's surface (p. 17)

latitude (LA • tuh • tood) imaginary lines on a globe that measure how far north or south a place is from the Equator (p. 14)

legislative branch (LEH • juhs • LAY • tihv BRANCH) the part of government that makes laws (p. 197)

longitude (LAHN • juh • tood) imaginary lines on a globe that measure distance east or west of the Prime Meridian (p. 14)

M

map legend (MAP LE • juhnd) the part of a map that tells what the symbols and colors on the map mean (p. 11)

map scale (MAP SKAYL) the part of a map that shows the distance between places (p. 13)

mass production (MAS pruh • DUHK • shuhn) making a large number of products quickly (p. 145)

midden (MIH • duhn) a trash pile of shells, bones, and other items (p. 31)

migrate (MEYE • grayt) to move from one place to another (p. 88)

militia (muh • LIH • shuh) a military unit (p. 60)

mission (MIH • shuhn) a settlement where religion was taught (p. 62)

moat (MOHT) a ditch filled with water that surrounds a fort (p. 58)

mobilize (MOH • buh • lyz) to get ready for action (p. 142)

*motivation (moh • tuh • VAY • shuhn) a reason to do something (p. 50)

N

natural resource (NA • chuh • ruhl REE • sawrs) a material that comes from Earth (p. 51)

New Deal (NOO DEEL) a plan to use government money to create jobs (p. 153)

O

*opinion (uh • PIHN • yuhn) what a person thinks about something (p. 59)

*organize (OR • guh • nyz) to put in order (p. 94)

P

palisade (pa • luh • SAYD) a high wooden fence (p. 31)

***perform** (puhr • FORM) to complete; to do (p. 89)

***permanent** (PUHR • muh • nuhnt) lasting (p. 56)

petition (puh • TIH • shuhn) a formal request made to a person of authority (p. 201)

pioneer (peye • uh • NIHR) the first of non-native people who settle a region (p. 99)

planter (PLAN • tuhr) a plantation owner (p. 93)

precipitation (prih • sih • puh • TAY • shuhn) any water that falls to Earth (p. 25)

***propose** (pruh • POHZ) to ask or suggest something (p. 95)

R

recession (rih • SEH • shuhn) a period of slow economic activity (p. 132)

recycle (ree • SY • kuhl) to make fit to use again (p. 200)

refugee (reh • fyoo • JEE) a person who flees a place to find safety or protection somewhere else (p. 183)

region (REE • juhn) an area with common features that make it different from other areas (p. 17)

relief (rih • LEEF) help sometimes given in the form of financial aid (p. 152)

reservation (reh • zuhr • VAY • shuhn) an area of land set aside for Native Americans (p. 94)

***rule** (ROOL) to govern or decide officially (p. 51)

S

secede (sih • SEED) to withdraw (p. 108)

segregation (seh • grih • GAY • shuhn) the practice of keeping racial groups separate (p. 118)

***setting** (seht • ting) a place or its surroundings (p. 157)

sharecropping (SHEHR • krah • ping) a system in which farmers rented land in return for a share of the crops that were grown on it (p. 117)

slavery (SLAY • vuh • ree) the practice of treating people as property and forcing them to work without pay (p. 53)

Glossary

stock (STAHK) a share in the ownership in a company (p. 150)

strait (STRAYT) a narrow passage of water between two larger bodies of water (p. 17)

***substitute** (SUHB • stuh • toot) to take the place of (p. 147)

***support** (suh • PORT) to help (p. 71)

T

technology (tek • NAH • luh • jee) the use of skills, ideas, and tools to meet people's needs (p. 103)

territory (TER • uh • tawr • ee) an area of land controlled by a nation (p. 92)

***theme** (THEEM) a main idea or topic (p. 192)

***toil** (TOY • uhl) to do hard and exhausting work (p. 100)

tourist (TUR • ihst) a person who travels for fun (p. 22)

transportation (trans • puhr • TAY • shuhn) the way in which people and goods are moved from one place to another (p. 103)

treaty (TREE • tee) an official agreement among countries (p. 70)

U

***unique** (yoo • NEEK) the only one of its kind (p. 182)

V

***vary** (VEHR • ee) to differ from (p. 30)

Index

This index lists many topics that appear in the book, along with the pages on which they are found. Page numbers after a *c* refer to a chart or diagram, after a *g* to a graph, after an *m* to a map, after a *p* to a photograph or a picture, and after a *q* to a quotation.

Index

Index

Index

Immigrants and immigration, 182–87
    arrival of, 138, *p138*, *p183*
    and citizenship, *p182*
    and cultural heritage, 184–85, *p184*, *p185*
    definition of, 135
    economic impact of, 186, *p186*
    languages of, 184, *c184*
    as refugees, 183
Imports, 194
Independence, 129, 141
Industry, 133–35
    cattle industry, 134, *m134*, *m190*, 191
    cigar industry, *m134*, 135
    citrus industry, *m134*, 135, 190, *m190*
    definition of, 129, 133
    phosphate industry, 133, *p133*, *m190*, 191, *p191*
    space industry, 188–89, *p188*, *p189*
    timber industry, 134, *m134*
    tourism industry, 192–93, *p192*, *m193*, *p193*
Integration, 129, 163
Interdependence, 179, 194
Intermediate directions, 13
Iowa, 107
Italy, 156

J

Jackson, Andrew, *p82*, 93, *p93*, 94
Jacksonville, Florida
    average temperatures in, *c25*
    and European explorers, *m58*, *p58*
    and railroad, 136
    tourist attractions in, 22, *m23*
Jacksonville Jaguars, 22, *m23*
Japan, 156
Jim Crow laws, 118
John Pennekamp Coral Reef State Park, 193
Johnson, James Weldon, 131, *c131*, *p131*, 164, *p165*
Judicial branch of state government, 197, *p197*, 198

Kennedy Space Center, 22, *p22*, *m23*, 189, 192
Key Deer, *p21*
Key Largo, Florida, 193
Key West, Florida
    average temperatures in, *c25*
    location of, *m23*
    and the Overseas Highway, 153
    and railroad, 137
King, Martin Luther, Jr., *p166*, 167
Kissimmee River, 21
Ku Klux Klan, 118

Lake Okeechobee
    flooding of, 149
    and the Kissimmee River, 21
    location of, *m23*
    size of, 20, *m20*
Landforms, 7, 17, 18
Languages, 184, *c184*
Latitude, *m14*, 14–15, *m15*
Laudonnière, René Goulaine de, 58
Lee, Robert E., 113, *p113*
Legislative branch of state government, 179, 197, *p197*, 198
Light bulbs, 147
Lightning, 26, *p26*
Lincoln, Abraham
    death of, 113
    election of 1860, 108, *p108*
Little Haiti, *p184*
Little Havana, 183, 185, *p185*
Local government, 198
Long houses, 30
Longitude, 7, *m14*, 14–15, *m15*

Index

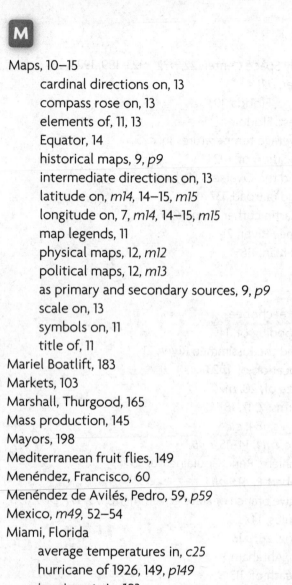

Index